Pitbull Harmony: The Art of Training and Understanding

Creating a Happy, Healthy, and Well-Balanced Canine Companion

Emily Turner

© Copyright 2024 - All rights reserved.

The content contained within this book may not be reproduced, duplicated or transmitted without direct written permission from the author or the publisher.

Under no circumstances will any blame or legal responsibility be held against the publisher, or author, for any damages, reparation, or monetary loss due to the information contained within this book, either directly or indirectly.

Legal Notice:

This book is copyright protected. It is only for personal use. You cannot amend, distribute, sell, use, quote or paraphrase any part, or the content within this book, without the consent of the author or publisher.

Disclaimer Notice:

Please note the information contained within this document is for educational and entertainment purposes only. All effort has been executed to present accurate, up to date, reliable, complete information. No warranties of any kind are declared or implied. Readers acknowledge that the author is not engaging in the rendering of legal, financial, medical or professional advice. The content within this book has been derived from various sources. Please consult a licensed professional before attempting any techniques outlined in this book.

By reading this document, the reader agrees that under no circumstances is the author responsible for any losses, direct or indirect, that are incurred as a result of the use of information contained within this document, including, but not limited to, errors, omissions, or inaccuracies.

Table of Contents

INTRODUCTION 5

CHAPTER I. Understanding Pitbulls 7

    Breed Characteristics and History 7

    Common Misconceptions 12

    Pitbull Myths vs. Reality 16

CHAPTER II. The Psychology of Pitbulls 21

    Understanding Canine Behavior 21

    Breed-specific Traits 25

    Building a Connection with Your Pitbull 29

CHAPTER III. Preparing for Pitbull Parenthood 33

    Setting up a Safe Environment 33

    Essential Supplies 38

    Choosing the Right Pitbull for You 43

CHAPTER IV. Basic Training Techniques 47

    Positive Reinforcement 47

    Clicker Training 52

    Basic Commands (Sit, Stay, Come) 56

CHAPTER V. Socializing Your Pitbull 60

    Importance of Socialization 60

    Introducing Your Pitbull to Other Pets 64

    Positive Interaction with Humans 68

CHAPTER VI. Addressing Behavioral Issues **73**
    Aggression and Fear 73
    Separation Anxiety 77
    Excessive Barking and Digging 81

CHAPTER VII. Physical and Mental Exercise **86**
    Daily Exercise Requirements 86
    Enrichment Activities 90
    Stimulating Your Pitbull's Mind 94

CHAPTER VIII. Health and Nutrition **99**
    Regular Vet Check-ups 99
    Choosing the Right Diet 103
    Common Health Issues in Pitbulls 108

CHAPTER IX. Grooming and Care **112**
    Bathing and Brushing 112
    Nail Trimming 115
    Dental Care 119

CHAPTER X. Pitbull Success Stories **123**
    Real-Life Stories of Well-Balanced Pitbulls 123
    Overcoming Challenges 126
    Celebrating the Bond Between Pitbulls and Owners .. 129

CONCLUSION **133**

INTRODUCTION

Welcome to "Pitbull Harmony: The Art of Training and Understanding - Creating a Happy, Healthy, Well- Balanced Canine Companion." This thorough manual is intended to help you navigate the world of responsible pitbull ownership, dispelling myths and misconceptions while offering invaluable insights into the unique characteristics of this beloved breed. As we embark on this journey together, we will focus on fostering a harmonious relationship between you and your pitbull through practical training, compassionate understanding, and a nurturing environment.

Pitbulls, often misunderstood due to misconceptions surrounding their temperament, are, in fact, loving, intelligent, and loyal companions. This e-book seeks to bridge the gap between perception and reality, providing knowledge about the breed's traits, history, and specific needs. By delving into the origins of pit bulls and understanding their breed-specific characteristics, we lay the groundwork for building a solid foundation for your relationship.

Training is an integral aspect of responsible pitbull ownership, and this e-book offers a comprehensive guide to positive reinforcement techniques tailored to the breed's unique temperament. From basic commands to more advanced skills, we'll explore the art of training, focusing on building trust, enhancing communication, and nurturing a strong bond between you and your pitbull. Additionally, we'll address common behavioral issues, offering practical advice on managing and overcoming challenges such as aggression, separation anxiety, and excessive barking.

Creating a happy, healthy, well-balanced pitbull extends beyond training to encompass their overall well-being. We'll explore providing a safe and enriching environment, understanding the importance of proper nutrition, exercise, and regular veterinary care. By embracing the principles of responsible ownership, you'll be equipped to meet your pitbull's physical and emotional needs, ensuring a fulfilling and joyful life for your canine companion.

Whether you're a first-time pitbull owner or a seasoned enthusiast, "Pitbull Harmony" is a holistic guide that empowers you with the knowledge and skills to cultivate a strong and harmonious bond with your pitbull. Together, we'll navigate the rewarding journey of pitbull ownership, dispelling myths, celebrating the breed's unique qualities, and laying the groundwork for a lifetime of love, understanding, and joy between you and your pitbull.

CHAPTER I

Understanding Pitbulls

Breed Characteristics and History

Each breed is unique because of its history and characteristics. Despite the negative stereotypes and myths surrounding Pitbulls, developing a more accurate and informed perspective necessitates understanding the traits and history of the breed.

Breed characteristics play a pivotal role in defining the nature and temperament of Pitbulls. Physically, Pitbulls are medium to large-sized dogs known for their muscular build, strength, and agility. Their short coat is smooth and lies close to the skin, requiring minimal grooming. The head is broad, often accompanied by a powerful jaw. While these physical traits may contribute to their intimidating appearance, it is crucial to recognize that their physical attributes do not solely determine a dog's behavior.

Temperament is a hallmark of breed characteristics, and Pitbulls are notably affectionate, loyal, and eager to please their owners. Despite the negative portrayals in the media, well-socialized and responsibly trained Pitbulls are known for their gentle and loving nature. Their loyalty to their human companions is often unwavering, and they thrive on positive interactions and a sense of belonging. This affectionate temperament, combined with their intelligence, makes them highly trainable and responsive to positive reinforcement.

Historically, pit bulls have roots in 19th-century England, where they were initially bred for bull-baiting and later used as catch dogs in hunting and farm work. The breeding aimed at combining the bulldog's strength with the terrier's agility and tenacity. These early Pitbulls were valued for their determination, fearlessness, and ability to work alongside humans. Their strength and athleticism made them well-suited for various tasks, including herding livestock and protecting property.

The breed's journey to the United States involved physical relocation and a shift in purpose. In America, Pitbulls were often used as farm dogs, helping with hunting, guarding livestock, and providing companionship to families. Their versatility and adaptability became evident as they transitioned from their historical roles in England to new responsibilities in the evolving American landscape.

One significant historical chapter for Pitbulls was their association with the American military during World War I. Sergeant Stubby, a Pit Bull mix, became a notable war hero and the most decorated dog in military history. Serving as a mascot and morale booster, Sergeant Stubby participated in 17 battles and earned several medals for his bravery and loyalty. This historical connection highlights the breed's ability to form strong bonds with humans and contribute positively to various societal roles.

Unfortunately, the reputation of Pitbulls took a turn for the worse in the mid-20th century as they became associated with dogfighting. Unscrupulous individuals exploited the breed's physical strength and tenacity for illegal and inhumane purposes. The media sensationalized stories, perpetuating negative stereotypes and contributing to the misconception that Pitbulls are inherently aggressive. It is critical to understand that a pit bull's behavior is shaped mainly by responsible ownership and that the behaviors of a small number of individuals do not define the breed as a whole.

In the 1980s and 1990s, Pitbulls faced increased stigmatization through breed-specific legislation (BSL), which targeted them based on their appearance rather than individual behavior. BSL imposed restrictions and bans on Pitbull ownership in certain areas, leading to discrimination against responsible owners and well-behaved dogs. The implementation of BSL underscored the importance of dispelling myths and promoting a more nuanced understanding of Pitbulls based on their actual characteristics and behavior.

In addition to being strong and agile, American Pit Bull Terriers are gregarious and friendly dogs. The American Staffordshire Terrier is a brilliant and adaptable dog that does well in agility and obedience trials, among other dog sports.

Pitbulls are a breed distinguished by qualities beyond looks and temperament, such as significant energy and a passion for physical activity. Because pit bulls enjoy playing and exercising, they need regular mental and physical stimulation opportunities. Playing games like fetch, agility training, or even swimming can help them stay healthy overall and avoid acting out of boredom.

Socialization is a critical component of Pitbull behavior and temperament. Early and positive socialization ensures that Pitbulls develop appropriate behaviors and interactions with other dogs, animals, and people. Despite their historical roles as working dogs, Pitbulls are generally friendly and can coexist harmoniously with proper introductions and positive experiences. Early socialization helps shape their behavior and contributes to their adaptability in various environments.

One of the persistent misconceptions about Pitbulls revolves around the idea of inherent aggression. The breed-specific traits and historical roles of Pitbulls must be distinguished from the actions of irresponsible owners who may encourage aggression for nefarious purposes. Numerous studies, including American Temperament Test Society assessments, consistently show that Pitbulls often score favorably in temperament evaluations. Responsible ownership, positive training methods, and early socialization play vital roles in shaping a pit bull's behavior and preventing aggression.

Another noteworthy aspect of the Pitbull breed is their intellect. Pitbulls are renowned for their aptitude for problem-solving and rapid learning. They are very trainable because of their intelligence and desire to please their owners. Pitbulls frequently perform exceptionally well in various dog sports, such as agility competitions, obedience trials, and therapeutic work. To satisfy their intellectual needs and stop boredom-related behaviors, providing mental stimulation through interactive games, puzzle toys, and training sessions is imperative.

Pitbulls are known for their intense prey drive, a characteristic from their past as hunters and catch dogs. This desire may affect their behavior, especially in the presence of smaller creatures. It takes early socialization and appropriate training to control their hunting drive and stop unwanted behaviors. Although each Pitbull may react differently to different situations, responsible ownership uses this instinct responsibly by harnessing and guiding it.

Despite the negative stereotypes perpetuated by media portrayals, Pitbulls often exhibit a gentle and affectionate nature, especially toward their human family members. Their loyalty and devotion are notable breed characteristics, and many Pitbulls are known for their patience and tolerance, particularly with children. Responsible owners who understand and appreciate these traits often find Pitbulls to be loving and loyal companions.

The appearance of Pitbulls is often a point of contention, with their distinctive physical characteristics contributing to negative perceptions. Pitbulls typically have a broad head, short coat, and strong jaw. Unfortunately, these physical traits have been unfairly associated with aggression, leading to breed-specific discrimination.

Dispelling myths about dogs' behavior requires responsible ownership and a grasp of breed-specific features beyond appearance. Acknowledging that a dog's outward appearance alone does not predict its conduct is essential.

The adaptability of Pitbulls to various environments and living conditions is a testament to their versatility as a breed. While they thrive in homes with active lifestyles and ample play and exercise opportunities, Pitbulls can adapt to urban or apartment living with sufficient mental and physical stimulation. Their resilience and ability to adjust to different situations highlight their versatility and make them suitable companions for various lifestyles.

In conclusion, understanding the breed characteristics and history of Pitbulls is essential for dispelling myths and fostering a more accurate perception of this diverse group of dogs. While certain physical traits may contribute to their historical roles and unique appearance, it is crucial to recognize that responsible ownership and proper training play pivotal roles in shaping a pit bull's behavior. Their affectionate nature, intelligence, loyalty, and adaptability make Pitbulls capable of forming deep bonds with their human companions. By challenging misconceptions and promoting responsible ownership, the true essence of Pitbulls as loving and loyal companions can shine through, contributing to a more positive image of this misunderstood breed.

Common Misconceptions

Unfortunately, common misconceptions about pit bulls contribute to the discrimination and unfavorable attitudes this diverse group of breeds—which includes the American Pit Bull Terrier, Staffordshire Bull Terrier, and American Staffordshire Terrier—faces. Pitbulls are renowned for their warmth, devotion, and flexibility, yet they are also commonly the focus of falsehoods that incite bigotry and anxiety. To encourage responsible ownership and constructive relationships within the community, these myths must be addressed, preconceived beliefs challenged, and a more accurate understanding of pit bulls developed.

One prevailing misconception about Pitbulls is the belief that they are inherently aggressive and dangerous. This stereotype is rooted in historical misuses of the breed for dogfighting, a cruel practice that exploited their strength and tenacity. However, separating irresponsible individuals' actions from the breed's inherent nature is crucial. Numerous studies, including American Temperament Test Society assessments, consistently show that Pitbulls often score favorably in temperament evaluations. The stigma associated with aggression overshadows the breed's natural affectionate temperament and loyalty to their human companions.

Another common misconception is the assumption that Pitbulls have a "locking jaw" mechanism, making them more dangerous during bites. This notion must be grounded in scientific evidence and more support from veterinary and canine experts. All dogs, regardless of breed, have jaws that function similarly, and the idea of a "locking jaw" is a myth. Pitbulls possess strong jaws, a historically valuable trait in their roles as hunters and catch dogs. Still, this characteristic does not make them uniquely dangerous or prone to locking onto their targets.

The misconception that Pitbulls are not suitable family pets is also widespread. In reality, many Pitbulls are known for their gentle and affectionate nature, making them excellent family companions. Their loyalty to their human family members, coupled with their patience and tolerance, especially with children, challenges the misconception that Pitbulls are not safe around families. Responsible ownership, proper socialization, and positive training play significant roles in shaping a pit bull's behavior and ensuring its compatibility with family life.

The word "Pitbull" is frequently used as a collective noun to refer to various breeds, which causes misunderstandings and confusion. As was previously noted, as every breed has unique qualities and attributes, grouping them under one word leads to confusion and oversimplification. For a more complex understanding of these breeds, it is imperative to acknowledge the variation within the "Pitbull" appellation.

A prevalent misconception is that Pitbulls have a higher likelihood of displaying aggression towards humans compared to other breeds. Credible studies do not support this belief, and in fact, Pitbulls often exhibit favorable temperaments in assessments. Aggression is not a breed-specific trait but rather a result of various factors, including temperament, socialization, training, and the owner's influence. Responsible ownership practices, early socialization, and positive reinforcement training are critical elements in preventing aggression in any dog breed, including Pitbulls.

Breed-specific legislation (BSL) is another misconception that negatively impacts Pitbulls. BSL often targets dogs based on physical appearance rather than individual behavior, leading to restrictions and bans in certain areas. Numerous studies have shown that BSL is ineffective in reducing dog bites or enhancing public safety. Education, responsible ownership, and community engagement are more effective strategies for promoting responsible dog ownership and ensuring public safety.

A widespread myth is that Pitbulls have a higher bite force than other dog breeds. This assertion is not supported by scientific evidence, and the idea that a dog's bite force correlates with its aggression is misleading. Various factors influence bite force, including jaw anatomy, size, and individual strength. Studies comparing the bite forces of different breeds have shown significant variations, and there is no conclusive evidence that Pitbulls possess an extraordinary or dangerous bite force.

The misconception that Pitbulls are not suitable for training or obedience work is contradicted by their intelligence and eagerness to please. Pitbulls are known for their quick learning abilities, problem-solving skills, and versatility in various canine activities. With positive reinforcement training methods, consistent guidance, and appropriate socialization, Pitbulls can excel in obedience trials, agility competitions, and even therapy work. Dismissing their trainability based on stereotypes overlooks the breed's intelligence and potential for positive contributions.

Pitbulls are often incorrectly labeled as unpredictable, and this misconception contributes to the fear and apprehension surrounding the breed. In reality, a well-socialized and responsibly trained Pitbull is generally predictable in its behavior, much like any other well-trained dog. Understanding and respecting a pit bull's personality, preferences, and experiences are essential for creating positive interactions. Fear-based stereotypes perpetuate a cycle of misunderstanding, hindering the potential for positive relationships between Pitbulls and the wider community.

One of the most damaging misconceptions is the belief that Pitbulls are more prone to "sudden aggression" or "snapping" without warning. This notion misrepresents the breed and unfairly portrays Pitbulls as unpredictable and dangerous. Dogs, including Pitbulls, communicate using body language and vocalizations to express their feelings and intentions. Sudden aggression is often a result of misinterpretation, fear, or external factors. Recognizing and understanding a pit bull's communication signals is crucial for preventing misunderstandings and fostering safe interactions.

Numerous examples of well-socialized and harmonious multi-pet households challenge the misconception that Pitbulls cannot coexist peacefully with other pets. While some Pitbulls may have a higher prey drive, early socialization and proper introductions can help them coexist with other animals. Individual temperament, training, and responsible ownership are pivotal in determining a Pitbull's compatibility with other pets. Assuming that all Pitbulls are inherently aggressive towards other animals oversimplifies their behavior and neglects the importance of individual variation.

The media's portrayal of pit bulls often contributes to misconceptions, emphasizing sensationalized stories and highlighting adverse incidents while neglecting positive examples. Breed-specific incidents are not exclusive to Pitbulls, and focusing on isolated incidents perpetuates bias. Responsible journalism should strive to provide a balanced and accurate representation of Pitbulls, showcasing their positive qualities, contributions, and the diversity within the breed. Positive media representation is crucial for challenging misconceptions and promoting a fair understanding of pit bulls.

In conclusion, addressing and dispelling common misconceptions regarding Pitbulls is essential for promoting responsible ownership, positive interactions, and fair treatment of these diverse and loving breeds. The negative stereotypes surrounding Pitbulls often stem from historical misuses, sensationalized media portrayals, and a lack of understanding of individual variation within the breed. By busting these misconceptions and advancing informed opinions, we can contribute to developing a more tolerant and compassionate atmosphere for Pitbulls in our local communities. Good interactions, education, and responsible ownership are crucial in dismantling the obstacles created by incorrect stereotypes and fostering a more accurate knowledge of Pitbulls.

Pitbull Myths vs. Reality

"Pitbull" often invokes solid emotions and opinions fueled by myths and misconceptions surrounding this misunderstood breed. However, the reality of pit bulls challenges these stereotypes, revealing a breed characterized by loyalty, affection, and versatility. By examining the true nature of Pitbulls, we can dispel the misconceptions surrounding them and foster a more accurate understanding of this diverse and misunderstood group of dogs.

One of the prevailing misconceptions about pit bulls is the notion of inherent aggression. Contrary to popular belief, aggression is not a breed-specific trait, and studies consistently demonstrate that well-socialized and responsibly trained Pitbulls can exhibit friendly and gentle behavior. Like any other dog breed, hereditary, environmental, and personal experiences significantly impact a pit bull's temperament. A pit bull's behavior can be greatly influenced by responsible ownership, appropriate training, and positive socialization, all of which help them develop into devoted and loving pets.

Another myth that persists in the public consciousness is the belief in a "locking jaw" mechanism attributed to Pitbulls. This notion, often cited as a reason for their perceived danger, lacks scientific basis. The anatomy of a Pitbull's jaw is no different from that of other dog breeds, and veterinary and canine experts have debunked claims of a locking mechanism. Pitbulls possess strong jaws, a characteristic historically valuable for their role as catch dogs. Still, this physical trait does not make them uniquely dangerous or prone to causing more severe bites than other breeds.

The stereotype that Pitbulls are not suitable family pets contradicts the reality experienced by countless families who share their lives with these dogs. Many Pitbulls are known for their gentle and affectionate nature, making them excellent family companions. Their loyalty to their human family members, coupled with their patience and tolerance, especially with children, challenges the misconception that Pitbulls are not safe around families. Responsible ownership practices, early socialization, and positive training play significant roles in shaping a pit bull's behavior and ensuring its compatibility with family life.

"Pitbull" is often used generically, contributing to oversimplification and misunderstanding. The label includes several distinct breeds, each with its characteristics and traits. Although they are all included in the Pitbull breed category, the American Pit Bull Terrier, Staffordshire Bull Terrier, and American Staffordshire Terrier each have distinctive characteristics that make grouping them all under the same category inaccurate. For a more complex understanding of these breeds, it is imperative to acknowledge the variation within the "Pitbull" appellation.

Breed-specific legislation (BSL) is a misguided response to misconceptions about Pitbulls and contributes to their unfair discrimination. BSL targets dogs based on physical appearance rather than individual behavior, leading to restrictions and bans in certain areas. This method unfairly singles out conscientious dog owners and well-behaved canines while ignoring the underlying reasons for occurrences involving dogs. Several studies have demonstrated that BSL has little effect in lowering the number of dog bites or improving public safety. More successful tactics for encouraging ethical dog ownership and guaranteeing public safety include education, responsible ownership, and community involvement.

The myth that Pitbulls have a higher likelihood of displaying aggression towards humans compared to other breeds is unsupported by credible studies. Pitbulls often exhibit favorable temperaments in assessments, and aggression is not a breed-specific trait. The focus should be on individual temperament, socialization, training, and responsible ownership rather than perpetuating stereotypes based on breed. By recognizing the individuality of each dog and addressing their needs accordingly, responsible ownership can prevent aggression in any breed, including Pitbulls.

Pitbulls, like any intelligent and trainable breed, should be more recognized regarding their capacity for training and obedience. The reality is that Pitbulls are known for their quick learning abilities, problem-solving skills, and eagerness to please. With positive reinforcement training methods, consistent guidance, and appropriate socialization, Pitbulls can excel in obedience trials, agility competitions, and even therapy work. Dismissing their trainability based on stereotypes overlooks the breed's intelligence and potential for positive contributions. Addressing misconceptions surrounding Pitbulls also involves debunking the idea that these dogs are unpredictable and dangerous. In reality, a well-socialized and responsibly trained Pitbull is generally predictable in its behavior, much like any other well-trained dog. Understanding and respecting a pit bull's personality, preferences, and experiences are essential for creating positive interactions. Fear-based stereotypes perpetuate a cycle of misunderstanding, hindering the potential for positive relationships between Pitbulls and the wider community.

Another damaging misconception is the belief that Pitbulls are more prone to "sudden aggression" or "snapping" without warning. This notion misrepresents the breed and unfairly portrays Pitbulls as unpredictable and dangerous. Dogs, including Pitbulls, communicate using body language and vocalizations to express their feelings and intentions. Sudden aggression is often a result of misinterpretation, fear, or external factors. Recognizing and understanding a pit bull's communication signals is crucial for preventing misunderstandings and fostering safe interactions.

Numerous examples of well-socialized and harmonious multi-pet households challenge the misconception that Pitbulls cannot coexist peacefully with other pets. While some Pitbulls may have a higher prey drive, early socialization and proper introductions can help them coexist with other animals. Individual temperament, training, and responsible ownership are pivotal in determining a Pitbull's compatibility with other pets. Assuming that all Pitbulls are inherently aggressive towards other animals oversimplifies their behavior and neglects the importance of individual variation.

Media portrayal of pit bulls often reinforces negative stereotypes, emphasizing sensationalized stories and highlighting adverse incidents while neglecting positive examples. Breed-specific incidents are not exclusive to Pitbulls, and focusing on isolated incidents perpetuates bias. Responsible journalism should strive to provide a balanced and accurate representation of Pitbulls, showcasing their positive qualities, contributions, and the diversity within the breed. Positive media representation is crucial for challenging misconceptions and promoting a fair understanding of pit bulls.

In conclusion, the reality of pit bulls challenges the prevailing stereotypes and misconceptions surrounding this diverse and loving group of breeds. By recognizing their loyalty, affectionate nature, and versatility, we can move beyond the unfounded fears that have led to breed-specific discrimination. Responsible ownership, education, and positive interactions are key elements in fostering a more accurate understanding of Pitbulls and dismantling the barriers created by unfounded stereotypes. As we embrace the reality of pit bulls, we contribute to a more inclusive and compassionate treatment of these misunderstood dogs within our communities.

CHAPTER II

The Psychology of Pitbulls

Understanding Canine Behavior

Understanding canine behavior is a complex and multifaceted endeavor that requires a nuanced approach to unravel the intricacies of the canine mind. As domesticated descendants of wolves, dogs have evolved alongside humans for thousands of years, forming intricate social structures and communication systems that distinguish them from their wild ancestors. Exploring canine behavior involves delving into various factors, including genetics, environment, training, and individual temperament.

Canine behavior is primarily influenced by genetics. Over many decades, certain dog breeds have been carefully cultivated to highlight qualities like guarding inclinations, retrieving prowess, or herding characteristics. These genetic predispositions contribute significantly to a dog's behavior, shaping their temperament and natural inclinations. For example, herding breeds may strongly desire to chase and control moving objects, while retrieving breeds may have an inherent love for fetching items.

The environment in which a dog is raised, and lives play a crucial role in shaping its behavior. Early experiences and socialization during a puppy's critical developmental period, typically between three and fourteen weeks, impact its behavior throughout life. Positive exposure to various people, environments, and stimuli during this period helps puppies develop into well-adjusted adults capable of navigating the complexities of the human world. Lack of socialization or negative experiences during this critical phase can result in behavioral issues, including fearfulness, aggression, or anxiety.

Training is another pivotal factor in understanding and shaping canine behavior. Dogs thrive on consistency, positive reinforcement, and clear communication with their human companions. Positive reinforcement, which involves rewarding desired behaviors, has been proven to be a highly effective training method. Conversely, punishment-based approaches can lead to fear, anxiety, and potentially aggressive responses. Canines have a great desire to please their owners, and a deep link and mutual understanding are fostered between canines and their human companions through good and gratifying training experiences.

Communication is a cornerstone of canine behavior, and dogs use a variety of signals to convey their emotions, intentions, and responses. Body language, vocalizations, and facial expressions are all components of canine communication. Understanding these cues is vital for interpreting a dog's mind and preventing misunderstandings leading to conflicts or stress. For example, a wagging tail may indicate excitement or friendliness, but it can also signal anxiety or fear if accompanied by other stress signals. Similarly, growling is a form of communication expressing discomfort or a desire to be left alone.

Social structure and hierarchy are integral to canine behavior, rooted in their ancestral wolf pack origins. While domestic dogs have adapted to living in human households, the influence of pack dynamics persists. Dogs often exhibit social behaviors that reflect their understanding of hierarchy and relationships within their human family or with other dogs. Recognizing and respecting a dog's need for structure and leadership can contribute to a harmonious and balanced relationship.

The concept of dominance has been a debate and misconception in understanding canine behavior. Traditional views often framed dogs as constantly vying for dominance within their households, promoting dominance-based training methods. However, modern studies and expert opinions challenge this notion, emphasizing the importance of positive reinforcement and cooperation rather than a dominance-submission paradigm.

Aggression is a behavior that requires careful consideration in the understanding of canine behavior. While aggression is a natural behavior in dogs, it can manifest for various reasons, including fear, territorial instincts, possessiveness, or frustration. Aggression should never be dismissed or trivialized, and addressing its root causes is crucial for creating a safe environment for the dog and its human companions. When dealing with aggression, consulting with a professional dog trainer or behaviorist is advisable, as they can assess the specific triggers and design a tailored behavior modification plan.

Canine behavior is also influenced by the dog's age and life stages. Puppies, for instance, may display exploration, playfulness, and teething behaviors. Adolescence brings about hormonal changes that can result in increased independence and testing of boundaries. Understanding the developmental stages of dog's aids in managing their behavior effectively and empathetically. Additionally, recognizing that older dogs may experience changes in behavior due to age-related factors, such as arthritis or cognitive decline, allows for appropriate adjustments in care and training.

Separation anxiety is prevalent in understanding canine behavior, especially for dogs left alone for extended periods. Destructive behaviors, excessive barking, or house soiling may result from separation anxiety. Preventing and addressing separation anxiety involves gradually acclimating dogs to being alone, providing mental stimulation, and ensuring they associate periods of solitude with positive experiences.

Canine behavior can be influenced by health-related factors as well. Behavior changes may result from underlying medical issues, physical discomfort, or pain. Unusual actions or an abrupt increase in aggression in a dog could be signs of a health problem. A dog's general health depends on routine veterinary examinations and quick reaction to any behavioral changes. Breeds play a significant role in shaping canine behavior, but it is essential to recognize the individuality of each dog. While certain breeds may predispose to specific behaviors, such as herding or retrieving, individual temperament varies widely. Factors such as early socialization, training, and the environment contribute significantly to a dog's behavior, emphasizing the importance of looking beyond breed stereotypes.

Understanding the role of fear in canine behavior is crucial for promoting positive interactions and preventing behavioral issues. Dogs consistently exposed to fear-inducing stimuli without proper desensitization and counter-conditioning may develop long-lasting anxieties. Recognizing and addressing fear-based behaviors with patience, positive reinforcement, and gradual exposure is essential for fostering a sense of security in dogs.

Providing mental stimulation for dogs is often underestimated in understanding canine behavior. Dogs are intelligent beings that require mental challenges to prevent boredom and related behavioral issues. Puzzle toys, interactive games, and training sessions engage a dog's cognitive abilities, promoting mental well-being. Mental stimulation is particularly crucial for breeds with high intelligence and energy levels, preventing the development of destructive behaviors born out of boredom.

Canine behavior is shaped by the bond between dogs and their human companions. The human-dog bond is reciprocal, with dogs offering unconditional love, loyalty, and friendship in return for care, attention, and positive interactions. Nurturing this bond through regular interaction, play, and shared activities strengthens the emotional connection between dogs and their owners.

In conclusion, understanding canine behavior is a multifaceted and dynamic process involving genetics, environment, training, communication, and individual temperament. Dogs are sentient beings with complex emotional lives, and interpreting their behaviors requires a blend of empathy, observation, and knowledge. Recognizing the influence of various factors on canine behavior enables responsible pet ownership and fosters positive relationships between dogs and their human companions. By approaching canine behavior with a holistic perspective, individuals can create environments that promote the well-being and happiness of their canine companions, ensuring a fulfilling and harmonious relationship for both parties.

Breed-specific Traits

Exploring the breed-specific traits of Pitbulls involves unraveling the unique characteristics that define these dogs, which are often misunderstood due to prevalent myths and misconceptions. Each of these breeds has its distinct traits, yet some commonalities contribute to the overall perception of Pitbulls.

One notable breed-specific trait of Pitbulls is their physical strength and muscular build. Pitbulls are medium- to large-sized dogs with robust and athletic appearances. Their well-defined muscles and powerful build reflect their historical roles as working dogs, particularly in activities such as bull-baiting and, later, as catch dogs in hunting and farm work. This physical strength is often misinterpreted, leading to the misconception that Pitbulls are inherently aggressive. In reality, their strength is a product of selective breeding for specific tasks rather than indicating a predisposition to violence.

Temperament is a crucial aspect of breed-specific traits, and Pitbulls are known for their affectionate nature and loyalty to their human companions. Despite the negative stereotypes perpetuated by media portrayals, well-socialized and responsibly trained Pitbulls can be incredibly gentle and loving. Pitbulls are enthusiastic to engage in various activities because they strongly desire to please their owners, and many are excellent in agility and obedience training. Strong relationships are frequently formed by the commitment and devotion of Pitbulls to their families, and they are well-known for being incredibly wonderful with kids, showing them patience and affection.

Another breed-specific trait of Pitbulls is their high energy levels and enthusiasm for physical activities. Pitbulls are an active and playful breed that thrives on regular exercise and mental stimulation. Playing fetch, agility training, or even swimming with them helps them stay physically fit and gives them something to do with their energy. This quality helps create a balanced and happy Pitbull when used appropriately. However, neglecting their activity requirements may lead to behaviors associated with boredom, highlighting how crucial an active lifestyle is for this species.

Socialization is a crucial aspect of Pitbull behavior that influences their interactions with other dogs and people. Early and positive socialization is vital for Pitbulls to develop appropriate behavior and prevent potential issues. Pitbulls are generally known for their friendly nature, and with proper introductions and positive experiences, they can coexist harmoniously with other pets and animals. However, due to their history as working dogs and innate prey drive, careful supervision is advised when introducing them to smaller pets.

The Pitbull's history as a fighting dog has impacted some breed-specific traits related to dog aggression. While it is true that specific individuals within the breed may display aggressive tendencies toward other dogs, it is essential to emphasize that aggression is not a universal trait for all Pitbulls. The American Temperament Test Society, which evaluates the temperament of various dog breeds, has consistently found that Pitbulls score favorably, often surpassing popular breeds like Beagles and Chihuahuas.

The intelligence of Pitbulls is another breed-specific trait that contributes to their versatility. Pitbulls are known for their quick learning abilities and problem-solving skills. Their passion to please and their intelligence make them very trainable. They do exceptionally well in various dog sports, such as agility trials, obedience contests, and therapeutic work. To satisfy their intellectual needs and stop boredom-related behaviors, providing mental stimulation through interactive games, puzzle toys, and training sessions is imperative.

Because of their ancestry as hunters and catch dogs, pit bulls are known for having a strong prey drive. This desire may affect how they behave, particularly in the presence of smaller creatures. Controlling their hunting instinct and ending undesirable behaviors requires early socialization and appropriate training. While Pitbull may respond to stimuli differently, a responsible owner can maintain and encourage this inclination.

A notable characteristic of Pitbulls is their distinctive appearance, often marked by a broad head, short coat, and a strong jaw. The appearance of Pitbulls has contributed to their negative image, as some people associate their physical traits with aggression. However, it is essential to recognize that physical appearance alone does not determine behavior, and the negative stereotypes surrounding Pitbulls based on their looks are unfounded. Responsible ownership and understanding breed-specific traits beyond appearance are crucial for dismantling misconceptions and fostering positive perceptions of Pitbulls.

The adaptability of Pitbulls to various environments and living conditions is another breed-specific trait worth noting. While they thrive in homes with active lifestyles, they can adapt to urban or apartment living with sufficient exercise and mental stimulation. Pitbulls are known for their resilience and ability to adjust to different situations, a testament to their versatility as a breed. Their adaptability and affectionate nature make them suitable companions for various families and individuals.

It is essential to approach the discussion of breed-specific traits with an understanding of the influence of individual variation. While specific characteristics may be shared among Pitbulls as a breed, individual dogs will exhibit unique personalities shaped by genetics, upbringing, and experiences. Responsible breeding practices, early socialization, positive training methods, and attentive care all foster desirable breed-specific traits in Pitbulls.

In conclusion, understanding the breed-specific traits of Pitbulls goes beyond debunking myths and stereotypes. It involves recognizing the multifaceted nature of these dogs, appreciating their historical roles, and acknowledging the individual variation within the breed. Pitbulls are characterized by their physical strength, affectionate temperament, high energy levels, and adaptability. When responsibly bred, trained, and socialized, Pitbulls can be outstanding companions, dispelling misconceptions and contributing positively to the diverse world of canine companionship.

Building a Connection with Your Pitbull

Understanding the distinctive characteristics of the breed, developing trust, and creating a happy atmosphere for the dog and its owner are all necessary to forge a solid and meaningful bond with your Pitbull. Each of these breeds shares specific characteristics that, when acknowledged and respected, can pave the way for a deep and fulfilling bond.

First and foremost, recognizing the breed-specific traits of Pitbulls is crucial for building a connection based on understanding and empathy. Pitbulls are often misunderstood due to prevalent myths and misconceptions, particularly regarding their temperament. Contrary to the negative stereotypes perpetuated by media portrayals, Pitbulls are known for their affectionate nature and loyalty to their human companions. They thrive on positive interactions, and their eagerness to please makes them receptive to forming strong bonds. Understanding their physical strength, high energy levels, and intelligence is essential for tailoring interactions and activities that align with their breed-specific traits.

Any genuine relationship with a dog, including a Pitbull, is built on trust. Positive and consistent interactions are essential to building trust, especially in the early phases of a relationship. Making trust and rewarding positive behavior with food, compliments, or play is known as positive reinforcement, and it's a very effective strategy for doing both. Pitbulls are happy to be praised, and this method strengthens the link between the dog and owner by encouraging cooperation and a sense of security. Socialization is critical to building a connection with a pit bull and plays a pivotal role in shaping its behavior. Early and positive socialization exposes Pitbulls to various people, environments, and stimuli, helping them develop into well-adjusted adults. Socialization enhances their adaptability and contributes to a more confident and friendly demeanor. Introducing your Pitbull to different experiences, such as meeting other dogs, encountering various sounds, and interacting with different people, helps them build positive associations and reduces the likelihood of fear-based behaviors.

Consistent and positive training is essential for mutual understanding and communication. Pitbulls are highly trainable with the correct attitude because they are intelligent and eager to please. Positive reinforcement training methods, where desired behaviors are rewarded, create a positive learning environment and strengthen the dog's and its owner's bond. Training sessions should be enjoyable and engaging, incorporating a mix of obedience commands, interactive games, and mental stimulation activities. This enhances the Pitbull's skills and deepens the connection through shared experiences and collaborative learning.

Creating a positive and enriching environment is paramount for building a solid connection with a pit bull. Dogs, including Pitbulls, thrive in environments where they feel secure, stimulated, and loved. Providing a comfortable and safe space and essential amenities such as proper nutrition, veterinary care, and grooming contributes to the dog's overall well-being. Regular exercise is necessary for Pitbulls, given their high energy levels. Engaging in daily walks, play sessions, and interactive toys fulfills their physical needs and strengthens the dog's and its owner's bond.

Time and quality interactions are fundamental for building a lasting connection with a Pitbull. Dogs, by nature, are social animals that crave companionship and attention. Spending quality time with your Pitbull through play, walks, or simple relaxation fosters a sense of connection and reinforces your bond. Positive interactions create positive associations; the more time invested in building a connection, the stronger the bond becomes. Understanding your Pitbull's individual preferences and personality allows for tailored interactions that resonate with their unique traits and preferences.

Pitbulls often face unfair discrimination due to breed-specific legislation (BSL) and negative stereotypes. Building a connection with your Pitbull involves advocating for the breed and challenging misconceptions. By being a responsible and conscientious Pitbull owner, you contribute to changing public perceptions and fostering a positive image of the breed. Engaging in community events, educating others about Pitbulls, and showcasing their positive attributes are ways to participate in advocating for the breed and dispelling myths actively.

Health and well-being are integral components of building a connection with your Pitbull. Regular veterinary check-ups, proper nutrition, and preventive care ensure that your Pitbull is in optimal health. Addressing health concerns promptly demonstrates your commitment to your dog's well-being and contributes to a longer and happier life together. Monitoring their weight, dental health, and grooming needs are essential aspects of responsible ownership that enhance the connection between you and your Pitbull.

Understanding the breed's history and heritage is another dimension that deepens the connection between Pitbull owners and their dogs. Pitbulls have a rich history as working dogs, participating in various roles such as hunting, herding, and even as therapy dogs. Recognizing and appreciating the breed's versatility and resilience adds a layer of understanding to the connection, highlighting the intrinsic value of Pitbulls beyond negative stereotypes. Learning about the breed's history can also provide insights into specific behaviors and traits rooted in their heritage.

Patience and empathy are virtues that play a crucial role in building a connection with a pit bull. Every dog has its personality, experiences, and responses to various situations. Pitbulls, in particular, may have faced challenges due to breed-specific stereotypes, and patience is necessary to help them overcome any fear or anxiety associated with these misconceptions. Empathy involves understanding the world from your Pitbull's perspective, acknowledging their needs, and responding to their emotions with kindness and compassion.

Responsible ownership is a cornerstone of building a connection with a Pitbull that goes beyond the individual bond. This involves complying with local regulations, providing proper training and socialization, and ensuring your dog's and the community's safety. Responsible Pitbull ownership extends to spaying or neutering to prevent overpopulation, ensuring adequate identification through tags or microchips, and advocating for the breed by promoting positive interactions and dispelling stereotypes.

In conclusion, building a connection with your Pitbull is a multifaceted journey that involves understanding breed-specific traits, establishing trust, and creating a positive environment. Recognizing the unique characteristics of Pitbulls, such as their affectionate nature, high energy levels, and intelligence, sets the stage for a deep and meaningful bond. Trust is cultivated through consistent positive interactions, socialization, and empathetic responses to the dog's needs. Positive training methods, a nurturing environment, and time spent together contribute to the strength of the connection. Responsible ownership, advocacy for the breed, and a commitment to the overall well-being of your Pitbull deepen the connection, creating a harmonious and fulfilling relationship between you and your loyal companion.

CHAPTER III

Preparing for Pitbull Parenthood

Setting up a Safe Environment

Creating a secure atmosphere for Pitbulls is crucial for their welfare and the harmony of their relationships with their owners and the neighborhood. Pitbulls frequently experience prejudice due to unfavorable preconceptions and breed-specific laws (BSL). For this reason, owners must provide a safe and encouraging environment that encourages responsible ownership and dispels myths.

Secure containment is critical to setting up a safe environment for Pitbulls. Pitbulls are known for their physical strength and agility, and providing secure fencing is essential to prevent escapes and ensure their safety. A sturdy, well-maintained fence, at least six feet tall, with no gaps or weaknesses, is recommended. Regular fence inspections for any wear or damage help maintain its effectiveness. Supervised outdoor activities reduce the risk of unintended incidents, especially in areas with high foot traffic or other animals.

Proper socialization is a critical factor in fostering a safe environment for Pitbulls. Early and positive exposure to various people, animals, and environments helps build confidence and reduces the likelihood of fear-based behaviors. Controlled introductions to other dogs, humans, and settings should be gradual, allowing the Pitbull to acclimate and form positive associations. This promotes a well-rounded and friendly dog and enhances safety during encounters with unfamiliar situations.

Educating the community and neighbors is a proactive measure to ensure a safe environment for Pitbulls.

Unfortunately, negative stereotypes and misconceptions surrounding the breed persist, leading to fear and prejudice. Open and honest communication about the breed's characteristics, dispelling myths, and showcasing responsible ownership practices can help change perceptions. Organizing community events, participating in dog-friendly activities, and encouraging positive interactions with your Pitbull contribute to fostering a supportive environment.

Another crucial aspect of creating a secure space for Pitbulls is proper identification. While collars with identification tags are standard, microchipping provides an added layer of protection. In the event of accidental escape or loss, microchips can significantly increase the chances of reunification with the owner. Ensuring that contact information associated with the microchip is up-to-date is essential for its effectiveness. Additionally, visible signage indicating the presence of a Pitbull on the property alerts visitors and passersby, promoting awareness and responsible interactions.

Regarding Pitbull safety, the significance of ethical breeding methods is immeasurable. Breeders who practice ethics put their dogs' health, temperament, and well-being first, helping to create individuals who are reliable and steady. Breeding responsibly lowers the risk of behavioral problems and genetic abnormalities, laying the groundwork for a safer and more dependable companion. Helping respectable breeders who put the breed's welfare first helps create a community of happy, healthy Pitbulls.

Establishing a safe environment for Pitbulls is primarily dependent on training. Positive reinforcement training methods, which involve rewarding desired behaviors, are highly effective in shaping their responses to various stimuli. Basic obedience commands, recall training, and leash manners improve control in public settings.

Consistency and patience during training sessions foster trust and cooperation, reinforcing a positive relationship between the owner and the Pitbull. Seeking professional training or behaviorist assistance for specific challenges ensures a tailored approach to individual needs.

Supervision is paramount in maintaining a safe environment, especially when Pitbulls interact with children, other pets, or unfamiliar situations. While Pitbulls are known for their affectionate nature, careful supervision is essential to prevent unintentional rough play or misunderstandings. Young children should be taught appropriate ways to interact with dogs, emphasizing the importance of gentle handling and respecting the dog's boundaries. Supervised introductions to other pets allow for positive interactions, reducing the risk of conflicts.

Pitbulls, like any dog breed, may display resource-guarding behaviors, and it is crucial to manage their environment accordingly. This involves providing a consistent feeding schedule, avoiding interference during meal times, and teaching the "drop it" or "leave it" commands. Educating family members and guests about the dog's boundaries and respecting their possessions helps prevent conflicts and ensures a safer living environment. These measures contribute to a harmonious relationship between the Pitbull and those sharing the household.

Routine veterinary care is fundamental to maintaining a safe environment for Pitbulls. Regular check-ups, vaccinations, and preventive measures against parasites and diseases are essential for their health. Prompt attention to signs of discomfort, illness, or behavioral changes ensures early intervention and appropriate care. Maintaining a record of vaccinations and veterinary visits also contributes to responsible ownership, demonstrating a commitment to the well-being of the Pitbull.

Building a positive and trusting relationship between Pitbulls and children requires intentional efforts. Educating children about dog behavior, teaching them to approach dogs calmly and avoid sudden movements, and establishing rules for respectful interactions contribute to a safe and enjoyable environment. When a dog exhibits symptoms of stress or discomfort, such as growling or averting eye contact, children should be trained to spot these indications and encouraged to give the animal space when necessary.

A safe and stimulating setting for Pitbulls must include both routine creation and mental stimulation. Regularity and predictability are what dogs love, so creating a regular daily routine might help them feel less stressed and anxious. Mentally stimulating activities like puzzle toys, interactive games, and training sessions prevent dogs from acting out of boredom and help foster a happy, healthy Pitbull.

Ensuring proper healthcare, including dental care, is crucial for maintaining a safe environment for Pitbulls. Regular dental hygiene practices, such as brushing teeth and providing dental chews or toys, prevent dental issues and contribute to overall well-being. Dental problems can lead to discomfort, affecting the dog's behavior and potentially leading to aggression. Proactive dental care measures promote a healthier and safer living environment for Pitbulls.

Spaying or neutering is an essential consideration in responsible Pitbull ownership. Beyond preventing unwanted litter, spaying or neutering can positively affect behavior, reducing the likelihood of certain aggressive tendencies. Additionally, spaying or neutering contributes to the dog's overall health and prevents reproductive-related issues. Discussing the appropriate timing and considerations for spaying or neutering with a veterinarian is essential in promoting a safe environment for Pitbulls.

Emergency preparedness is a vital aspect of responsible ownership and contributes to the safety of Pitbulls. Familiarizing yourself with local emergency resources, including veterinary clinics, animal shelters, and pet-friendly evacuation centers, ensures quick and effective responses in unforeseen circumstances. A designated emergency kit with essential supplies, medical records, and contact information facilitates a swift and organized response in times of need.

In conclusion, setting up a safe environment for Pitbulls involves a comprehensive and proactive approach that addresses various aspects of their care and interactions. Secure containment, proper socialization, responsible breeding practices, and positive training methods create a safe and harmonious living space. Educating the community, promoting awareness, and challenging breed-specific stereotypes further enhance the safety of Pitbulls within their communities. A commitment to responsible ownership, routine veterinary care, and emergency preparedness ensures that Pitbulls thrive in an environment that prioritizes their well-being, fostering positive relationships with their owners and the broader community.

Essential Supplies

It is crucial to ensure that you have the tools required for the upkeep and welfare of your Pitbull. Combinations of the American Pit Bull Terrier, Staffordshire Bull Terrier, and American Staffordshire Terrier result in the breed referred to as "Pitbull." Each breed in this group has distinctive qualities, and providing for their basic needs raises their comfort level, overall well-being, and quality of life. Starting with the basics, a proper and comfortable shelter is essential for your Pitbull. While many Pitbulls are kept as indoor pets, having a dedicated space to rest and seek shelter is necessary. This may include a cozy dog bed, crate, or designated area in your home where your Pitbull can feel secure. If your Pitbull spends time outdoors, providing a well-insulated doghouse with proper ventilation is crucial, ensuring they are protected from the elements.

Nutritious and well-balanced food is a cornerstone of Pitbull care. High-quality dog food for their age, size, and activity level is essential. Discuss your Pitbull's diet needs with your veterinarian to maintain maximum health. Your dog may benefit from kibble, wet food, or both. Keep a clean, easily accessible water bowl on hand at all times because staying adequately hydrated is just as vital.

For Pitbulls, ensuring correct identification is an essential safety precaution. Collars with ID tags that show your contact details are crucial in case your Pitbull goes missing. Furthermore, microchipping gives your Pitbull a permanent form of identification, improving the likelihood of a safe reunion if other people find your dog. It's essential to keep this information current, particularly if you relocate or update your contact information.

Grooming supplies are essential for maintaining your Pitbull's hygiene and appearance. Pitbulls have short coats that require regular brushing to remove loose hair and minimize shedding. A grooming brush suitable for their coat type, nail clippers, canine-friendly toothpaste, and a toothbrush are essential. Regular grooming keeps your Pitbull looking and feeling their best and helps prevent potential health issues.

Collars and leashes are fundamental tools for managing and controlling your pit bull, especially during walks or outings. Choose a sturdy and well-fitting collar with an identification tag and a leash suitable for their size and strength. Proper leash training is essential for Pitbulls, as their physical strength can make them challenging to control without the right equipment and guidance.

Not only do toys provide entertainment value, but they also enhance your pit bull's brain stimulation and general well-being. Pitbulls are known for their strong jaws and love for chewing, so providing durable chew toys helps satisfy this instinct while preventing destructive chewing on household items. Interactive toys, such as puzzle feeders or dispensing treats, engage their minds and keep them mentally stimulated.

Regular exercise is crucial for Pitbulls due to their high energy levels and athletic nature. A sturdy and well-fitting harness is an excellent option for walks and outdoor activities, distributing the force evenly across the chest and shoulders. Consider a long leash for off-leash play in a secure area. Interactive play, such as fetch or tug-of-war, provides physical exercise and bonding time with your pit bull.

Maintaining your Pitbull's health includes regular veterinary care. A first aid kit for dogs is a valuable supply to have on hand for minor injuries or emergencies. Essential items such as bandages, antiseptic wipes, tweezers for removing splinters or ticks, and any medications your veterinarian prescribes contribute to your Pitbull's well-being. Having a reliable and accessible emergency veterinary contact number is also essential in case of unexpected health issues.

Quality feeding bowls are essential for Pitbulls to ensure a clean and convenient eating experience. Stainless steel or ceramic bowls are durable, easy to clean, and resistant to bacterial growth. Elevated bowls can benefit larger Pitbulls or those with specific health conditions, promoting better posture during meals. Regularly cleaning and sanitizing your Pitbull's feeding bowls contribute to their overall health and hygiene.

Training supplies are crucial for teaching your Pitbull obedience and appropriate behavior. High-value treats, a clicker for positive reinforcement training, and a durable training leash are essential tools. Consistent and positive training sessions enhance your Pitbull's behavior and strengthen the bond between you and your dog. A comfortable and well-fitting training harness can be helpful in control during training sessions.

Proper waste disposal is a responsible aspect of Pitbull ownership. Poop bags, a sturdy poop scooper, and a designated waste disposal system help keep public spaces clean during walks or outings. Responsible waste management positively affects Pitbull owners and contributes to the community's overall perception of the breed. Always carry waste disposal supplies and promptly clean up after your Pitbull to maintain a clean and pleasant environment.

Dental care supplies contribute to your Pitbull's oral health. Canine-friendly toothpaste and a dog toothbrush help prevent dental conditions such as tartar and plaque accumulation. Regular dental care is crucial for Pitbulls, as they are prone to dental problems, and poor oral hygiene can impact their overall health. Incorporating dental care into your routine contributes to your Pitbull's well-being and prevents potential dental-related discomfort.

Comfortable and weather-appropriate clothing may be necessary for Pitbulls, particularly in colder climates.

While some Pitbulls have a naturally dense coat, others may benefit from the warmth a dog sweater or jacket provides during colder seasons. Additionally, protective gear, such as booties, can help shield their paws from extreme temperatures, rough terrain, or harmful substances during walks.

Pitbulls, like all dogs, benefit from routine veterinary check-ups and preventive healthcare. Regular vaccinations, parasite prevention, and dental examinations are essential to maintaining their overall health. Veterinary care addresses existing health issues and allows for early detection of potential concerns, ensuring timely intervention and optimal well-being for your Pitbull.

Choose a bed that accommodates their size and allows for stretching and curling up comfortably. Orthopedic or memory foam beds are excellent options for older Pitbulls or those with joint issues. Providing a comfortable sleeping space contributes to your Pitbull's overall comfort and well-being.

Pitbulls, like many dogs, may experience anxiety or stress in certain situations. Calming products, such as anxiety wraps, pheromone diffusers, or containing supplements, can help alleviate stress and promote a sense of security for your pit bull. Speak with your veterinarian to find the best soothing products for your dog, especially during thunderstorms, fireworks, or travel.

Your Pitbull's health and well-being depend on you keeping their environment tidy and sanitary. Odors, stains, and cleanliness can be controlled with dog-safe cleaning products, including grooming wipes, pet-friendly disinfectants, and stain removers. Your Pitbull will live in a safe and healthy environment if their living area, feeding bowls, and grooming supplies are cleaned regularly.

A sturdy and well-ventilated travel crate is essential for Pitbull owners transporting their dogs. Whether for car travel or flying a secure and appropriately sized crate provides a safe space for your Pitbull during journeys. Familiarizing your Pitbull with the crate and ensuring it meets safety standards contribute to stress-free and secure travel experiences.

The love and attention you provide are the most essential supplies for your pit bull. Dogs, including Pitbulls, thrive on companionship, positive interactions, and a strong bond with their owners. Spending quality time with your Pitbull through play, walks, and relaxation fosters a deep connection and improves their emotional well-being. Your presence and affection are the most valuable supplies contributing to your Pitbull's happiness and contentment.

In conclusion, ensuring you have the essential supplies for your Pitbull is a fundamental aspect of responsible ownership. From necessities like shelter and nutritious food to grooming tools, training supplies, and healthcare items, each supply plays a role in promoting the well-being of your pit bull. By offering a secure, cozy, and engaging setting, you support the general well-being, contentment, and favorable opinion of Pitbulls in your neighborhood.

Choosing the Right Pitbull for You

Selecting a Pitbull as a companion is a decision that requires careful consideration, responsible planning, and a commitment to providing the best possible life for your new four-legged family member. Potential Pitbull owners must prioritize accountable ownership practices, understand the breed's needs, and make informed choices that align with their lifestyle to ensure a harmonious and fulfilling relationship. This guide thoroughly explains all the essential aspects to consider while selecting the ideal Pitbull.

First and foremost, understanding the breed characteristics is crucial in making an informed decision. Pitbulls are medium to large-sized dogs known for their muscular build, strength, and agility. Their short coat is easy to maintain, and they exhibit loyalty, affection, and intelligence. Despite the negative stereotypes, well-socialized and responsibly trained Pitbulls often display a gentle and loving nature. It's essential to recognize that various factors, including genetics, environment, and owner influence, shape a dog's behavior. Choosing the right Pitbull involves looking beyond physical appearance and understanding the breed's temperament, energy levels, and overall compatibility with your lifestyle.

Consideration of your living situation is paramount when choosing a pit bull. Whether you reside in an apartment, a suburban home, or a rural setting, understanding the breed's exercise needs is crucial. Pitbulls are known for their high energy levels and enthusiasm for physical activities. Frequent exercise is vital for their cerebral stimulation as well as physical wellness. To keep your pit bull happy psychologically and physically, owners should be ready to participate in regular activities like walks, playtime, and interactive games. Consider whether your daily schedule and living area can support a Pitbull's demand for regular exercise and mental stimulation before introducing one into your house.

Pitbulls thrive on human companionship, and their loyalty makes them excellent family pets. However, it's essential to consider the dynamics of your household when choosing a pit bull. Assess family members' age, temperament, and activity levels, including children and pets. Pitbulls are generally affectionate and patient, making them suitable for families. Early socialization and positive interactions with children and animals are crucial for fostering a harmonious relationship. A gradual and supervised introduction is recommended to ensure compatibility if you have existing pets. Additionally, educating all family members about responsible dog ownership and proper interactions contributes to a positive and safe environment for everyone.

Another crucial aspect of responsible Pitbull ownership is recognizing the importance of proper training and socialization. Pitbulls are very trainable because of their intelligence and desire to please. Regularly using positive reinforcement-based training techniques helps guarantee a well-mannered dog by shaping desired behaviors. From an early age, socialization involves exposing the pit bull to various situations, humans, and other animals to promote adaptability and prevent behavioral problems. Enrolling in puppy training classes or speaking with a qualified dog trainer will help lay the groundwork for a good foundation of obedience and manners.Health considerations should be your top priority while choosing the perfect Pitbull for you. Breeders who adhere to responsible breeding practices prioritize the health and wellbeing of their dogs, use genetic testing and thorough health checks to lower the probability of inherited illnesses. When selecting a Pitbull, inquire about the breeder's health practices, including vaccinations, deworming, and veterinary care. A reputable breeder documents the dog's health history, ensuring transparency and accountability. Potential owners should also be prepared for routine veterinary check-ups and preventive treatment and be aware of prevalent health issues in the breed, such as allergies and hip dysplasia.

Another admirable choice is to adopt a Pitbull from a shelter or rescue group. Many Pitbulls in shelters are loving, well-socialized dogs seeking a second chance at a happy life. Shelters often conduct behavioral assessments to help match dogs with suitable homes. Adopting from a rescue allows you to provide a home for a dog in need while contributing to the overall welfare of the breed. However, gathering information about the dog's background, including any history of abuse or neglect, is essential to ensure a smooth transition into the new environment. Shelters and rescue organizations are valuable resources for finding the right Pitbull for your family and lifestyle.

Understanding your area's legal aspects and breed-specific legislation (BSL) is crucial when considering a pit bull. Unfortunately, Pitbulls face discrimination in some regions, with restrictions and bans based on their physical appearance rather than individual behavior. Familiarize yourself with local regulations, and be prepared to adhere to any specific requirements for Pitbull ownership. Responsible ownership, including leash laws, proper containment, and adherence to local ordinances, helps counteract negative perceptions and promotes a positive image of Pitbulls within the community.

Financial preparedness is an often overlooked but critical factor in responsible Pitbull ownership. The costs associated with caring for a dog include veterinary expenses, food, grooming supplies, training classes, and unexpected medical emergencies. Budgeting for these expenses ensures that you can provide your Pitbull with the necessary care and support throughout their life. Additionally, considering the long-term commitment involved in dog ownership, including potential changes in financial circumstances, is critical to the dog's and the owner's health.

Responsible breeders and reputable rescue organizations play pivotal roles in helping prospective Pitbull owners make informed decisions. When seeking a breeder, research their reputation, ask for references, and visit their facilities to ensure ethical breeding practices. Reputable breeders prioritize their dogs' health, temperament, and overall well-being. Rescue organizations should provide detailed information about the dog's history, behavior assessments, and any known health issues. Responsible breeders and rescues are invested in the welfare of the dogs they place and often establish ongoing relationships with adopters to provide guidance and support.

In conclusion, you are choosing the right Pitbull for you. It is a complex choice that calls for thoughtful thought, prudent preparation, and a dedication to giving your new dog the best life possible. Understanding the breed characteristics, evaluating your living situation, considering family dynamics, prioritizing training and socialization, addressing health considerations, and being aware of legal aspects are all essential factors in the decision-making process. Whether you work with a responsible breeder or adopt from a shelter, the key is to prioritize the Pitbull's well-being and contribute positively to the overall perception of this misunderstood breed. Responsible ownership practices, informed decision-making, and a genuine commitment to your Pitbull's welfare create a foundation for a rewarding and fulfilling relationship between you and your new four-legged friend.

CHAPTER IV

Basic Training Techniques

Positive Reinforcement

Positive reinforcement training stands as a beacon of effective and humane methods in shaping the behavior of dogs, including the much-maligned Pitbulls. This approach to training focuses on rewarding desired behaviors, using positive stimuli such as treats, praise, or play to reinforce actions that the trainer wants to encourage. In the case of Pitbulls, notorious for their strength and tenacity, positive reinforcement is an effective training method and a powerful tool for fostering a strong bond between the owner and the dog. This essay explores the principles and benefits of positive reinforcement training for Pitbulls, highlighting how this approach can contribute to their well-being, sociability, and positive perception within the community.

Positive reinforcement training is rooted in the fundamental principle of reinforcing behaviors that an owner wants to see more frequently. When a dog exhibits a desirable behavior, such as sitting, staying, or coming when called, the trainer immediately rewards the dog with a positive stimulus. This reinforcement strengthens the connection between the behavior and the reward, making it more likely for the dog to repeat the action in the future. Pitbulls, known for their intelligence and eagerness to please, respond exceptionally well to positive reinforcement, making it an ideal training method for this breed.

Treating as a primary form of positive reinforcement is a common and effective practice in training Pitbulls. High-value treats, such as small pieces of meat or special dog treats, are a powerful motivator for Pitbulls. The immediacy of the reward is crucial for the dog to associate the treat with the specific behavior, reinforcing the positive action. Treats encourage desired behaviors and establish a positive association between training sessions and enjoyable experiences for the pit bull.

In addition to treats, verbal praise, and affection are vital components of positive reinforcement training for Pitbulls. Dogs naturally seek approval and affection from their owners, and Pitbulls are no exception. Verbal cues such as "good boy" or "well done," accompanied by petting or a belly rub, provide positive feedback and strengthen the bond between the owner and the Pitbull. Consistent and genuine praise creates a positive training environment, fostering a sense of trust and cooperation between the dog and its owner.

To implement positive reinforcement effectively, timing is of the essence. The required behavior must occur before the reward, which allows the Pitbull to connect the action and the positive consequence. This instant feedback helps the dog understand what is expected, making the training process more efficient and reinforcing the desired behaviors more effectively. Consistency in timing and rewards is critical to building a solid foundation for positive reinforcement training.

One of the significant advantages of positive reinforcement training is its focus on encouraging and reinforcing desired behaviors rather than punishing unwanted behaviors. Pitbulls, like any other breed, respond better to positive reinforcement than to punishment-based methods. Punishment, such as physical corrections or harsh reprimands, can lead to fear, anxiety, and aggression in dogs. Positive reinforcement, on the other hand, creates a positive association with training and fosters a cooperative and willing attitude in pit bulls.

Pitbulls that exhibit common behavioral problems, including jumping, pulling on the leash, or excessive barking, can be trained with positive reinforcement. For example, when teaching a Pitbull to walk politely on a leash, the trainer can reward the dog for walking calmly beside them and withhold treats when the dog pulls. This approach helps the Pitbull understand the desired behavior and encourages them to walk nicely on the leash to earn the reward. Positive reinforcement provides a constructive and enjoyable way to address behavioral challenges, promoting a positive relationship between the owner and the dog.

Socialization is a crucial aspect of a pit bull's development, and positive reinforcement significantly impacts how they interact with people and other dogs. Early and positive exposure to various environments, people, and animals helps prevent fear and aggression in Pitbulls. Positive reinforcement during socialization reinforces positive behaviors and allows the Pitbull to associate new experiences with positive outcomes. Treats, praise, and affection can reward calm and friendly behavior during interactions, contributing to developing a well-mannered and friendly Pitbull.

One of the misconceptions about Pitbulls is that they are inherently aggressive, and positive reinforcement training provides an effective means to challenge and dispel this stereotype. By focusing on reinforcing positive behaviors and encouraging sociability, owners can demonstrate the true nature of Pitbulls as affectionate and gentle companions. Positive reinforcement helps create positive associations with people and other animals, contributing to a more accurate and positive perception of Pitbulls within the community.

Positive reinforcement training is not limited to basic obedience commands; it extends to addressing more complex behaviors and activities. With their intelligence and agility, Pitbulls excel in various canine activities, including agility training, obedience trials, and even therapy work. Positive reinforcement can be applied to teach advanced commands and tricks and engage the Pitbull in mentally stimulating activities. The versatility of positive reinforcement makes it a valuable tool for owners who want to explore and enhance their Pitbull's capabilities beyond basic obedience.

The positive reinforcement method also gives owners the ability to deal with behaviors in Pitbulls that stem from fear and anxiety. Positive reinforcement is a valuable tool in helping Pitbulls overcome their concerns, regardless of the source of their anxiety. This includes fears rooted in traumatic experiences in the past as well as those associated with loud noises and unfamiliar places. By rewarding calm and relaxed behavior in the presence of feared stimuli, owners can gradually desensitize their Pitbull and create positive associations, contributing to a more balanced and confident demeanor.

Building a strong bond between the owner and the Pitbull is a central goal of positive reinforcement training. The mutual trust and respect established through positive interactions and rewards create a positive and cooperative relationship. Pitbulls, known for their loyalty, respond well to owners who use positive reinforcement, fostering a deep connection and a sense of partnership. The bond formed through positive reinforcement extends beyond training sessions, influencing the overall well-being and happiness of the Pitbull.

It is essential to tailor positive reinforcement training to the individual personality and preferences of the Pitbull. Each dog is unique, and what may be a high-value reward for one Pitbull may be less appealing to another. Understanding the Pitbull's preferences and adjusting the rewards accordingly ensures that the positive reinforcement is effective and enjoyable for the dog.

Some Pitbulls may be motivated by treats, while others may respond better to praise or play. Being attuned to the individual needs of the Pitbull enhances the success of positive reinforcement training.

While positive reinforcement is a powerful and humane training method, it is not a one-size-fits-all solution. Owners should know their Pitbull's strengths, challenges, and limitations. Positive reinforcement may not address all behavioral issues effectively, but consulting a professional dog trainer or behaviorist can provide additional guidance and support. Combining positive reinforcement with other training methods and tools, such as proper equipment and structured routines, contributes to a comprehensive and practical training approach.

In conclusion, positive reinforcement training stands as a compassionate and effective method for shaping the behavior of Pitbulls, fostering a strong bond between owners and their canine companions. This approach emphasizes reinforcing desired behaviors through rewards, creating a positive association with training, and promoting a cooperative attitude in Pitbulls. Positive reinforcement is particularly well-suited for Pitbulls, known for their intelligence, eagerness to please, and affectionate nature. Owners can foster positive relationships, dispel unfavorable preconceptions, and improve the general wellbeing and public impression of Pitbulls by providing food, verbal praise, and affection. Building a solid and enduring relationship between Pitbulls and their owners can be achieved through training techniques such as favorable reinforcement.

Clicker Training

Dog training with clicker training has become a popular and very successful technique. With their intellect, quickness, and desire to please, Pitbulls are especially suitable for this kind of positive reinforcement. This section delves into the principles and benefits of clicker training with Pitbulls. It explores how this precise and positive approach can enhance their learning, strengthen the bond between owners and dogs, and contribute to a positive perception of this often-misunderstood breed within the community.

At the core of clicker training is operant conditioning, a learning theory that involves associating behaviors with consequences. The clicker serves as a precise and consistent marker, signaling to the Pitbull that the specific behavior exhibited at the exact moment of the click is the one being reinforced. This immediacy allows clear communication between the trainer and the dog, facilitating a quicker understanding of the desired behaviors. Pitbulls, known for their sharp learning abilities, respond exceptionally well to the precision and consistency provided by clicker training.

The clicker is a neutral stimulus, devoid of emotion or tone, eliminating the potential for communication confusion. Unlike verbal cues that vary in tone or intensity, the clicker consistently produces the same sharp and distinct sound. This neutrality helps prevent miscommunication and allows Pitbulls to focus on the specific behavior being reinforced rather than being influenced by the trainer's tone or body language. The precision of the clicker makes it a valuable tool in shaping behaviors with clarity and accuracy.

Positive reinforcement lies at the heart of clicker training, emphasizing rewards to strengthen desired behaviors. The clicker marks the exact moment the behavior occurs, and the Pitbull is immediately rewarded with a treat, praise, or play. This immediate reinforcement creates a strong association between the behavior and the positive outcome, making it more likely for the Pitbull to repeat the action in the future. The positive nature of clicker training fosters a cooperative and eager-to-learn attitude in Pitbulls, contributing to a favorable rapport between the dog and the trainer.

Clicker training's adaptability in teaching a broad range of behaviors and commands is one of its most important benefits. Through clicker training, which covers everything from basic obedience commands like sit, stay, and come to more complex tricks and jobs, owners may effectively interact with their Pitbulls. Trainers can more easily shape complex activities using the clicker's accuracy to record and reinforce particular behavioral moments. Clicker training offers Pitbulls an easy and gratifying approach to becoming proficient in learning and performing tricks, agility routines, and object retrieval.

Clicker training efficiently addresses behavioral challenges commonly associated with Pitbulls, such as leash pulling, jumping, or excessive barking. The precision of the clicker allows trainers to capture and reinforce moments of calm and desired behavior, providing an alternative to unwanted actions. For example, when teaching a pit bull to walk calmly on a leash, the clicker can mark and reinforce moments of loose leash walking. This constructive method keeps a cooperative, upbeat training atmosphere while addressing behavioral issues.

A pit bull's socialization is essential to its development, and clicker training helps mold favorable connections with people and other canines. Clicker training during socialization reinforces desirable behaviors, creating positive associations with new experiences. For example, the clicker can mark and support calm and friendly interactions with unfamiliar dogs or people. This positive reinforcement builds confidence and sociability in Pitbulls, contributing to their well-mannered and well-adjusted behavior in various social settings.

The clicker bridges the behavior and the reward, allowing trainers to capture and reinforce behaviors in real time. This immediacy is particularly beneficial in complex training scenarios or when working with Pitbulls on advanced commands. The precise timing of the clicker enables trainers to communicate with the Pitbull without delay, creating a clear connection between the behavior and the subsequent reward. The speed and accuracy of clicker training make it an ideal method for teaching Pitbulls intricate tasks or behaviors that require precise timing.

Clicker training enhances the communication and understanding between the owner and the Pitbull. The clicker's clarity reduces confusion, allowing the Pitbull to quickly grasp the connection between their actions and the desired outcomes. This heightened understanding fosters a stronger bond between the trainer and the dog, as the Pitbull learns to trust and engage with the owner positively and cooperatively. The positive reinforcement nature of clicker training contributes to a harmonious relationship based on trust, mutual respect, and shared positive experiences.

Pitbulls, like any intelligent and trainable breed, thrive on mental stimulation and engagement. Clicker training offers a mentally enriching experience for Pitbulls, challenging their cognitive abilities and problem-solving skills. The process of learning new behaviors and tasks through clicker training provides Pitbulls with mental stimulation, preventing boredom and associated behavioral issues. Engaging in clicker training sessions also provides an outlet for the Pitbull's energy and curiosity, contributing to their overall well-being and contentment.

The positive and precise nature of clicker training makes it an ideal method for building a positive image of Pitbulls within the community. By showcasing their intelligence, trainability, and eagerness to learn through positive reinforcement, Pitbull owners can challenge negative stereotypes and misconceptions surrounding the breed. Public demonstrations or participation in canine events where Pitbulls display the skills they learned through clicker training contribute to a more accurate and positive perception of the breed. Positive interactions between well-behaved Pitbulls and the community help dispel unfounded fears and contribute to a more inclusive view of these dogs.

While clicker training is a powerful tool, it is essential to consider each Pitbull's individual needs and preferences. Some dogs may be more sensitive to the clicker's sound, while others may find it particularly motivating. Owners should observe their Pitbull's reactions and adjust the training approach accordingly. Additionally, pairing the clicker with various rewards, including treats, praise, and play, ensures the training remains enjoyable and engaging for the Pitbull.

In conclusion, clicker training offers a positive, precise, and versatile approach to training Pitbulls, capitalizing on their intelligence, eagerness to please, and agility. This method, rooted in positive reinforcement and operant conditioning principles, creates a clear communication channel between the trainer and the Pitbull. The clicker is a powerful tool for shaping behaviors, teaching new commands, and addressing behavioral challenges positively and effectively. Beyond training, clicker training contributes to the mental stimulation, well-being, and positive perception of Pitbulls within the community. By embracing clicker training, owners can foster a strong bond with their Pitbulls while challenging negative stereotypes and showcasing their true potential as intelligent, trainable, and loving companions.

Basic Commands (Sit, Stay, Come)

Training a Pitbull in basic commands is foundational in fostering a well-behaved and harmonious relationship between the owner and their canine companion. In contrast to popular belief, Pitbulls are highly trainable, clever, and eager to please dogs. This section explores the importance of basic command training for Pitbulls, focusing on the basic commands of sit, stay, and come. This training establishes essential behaviors for day-to-day living and contributes to the overall well-being, safety, and positive perception of Pitbulls within the community.

The command "sit" is one of the first and most crucial behaviors to teach a Pitbull. Teaching a Pitbull to sit is a foundational command that can be applied in various situations, from greeting guests to preventing jumping or excessive excitement. When preparing a Pitbull to sit, positive reinforcement—such as praise or treats—must be used to acknowledge and encourage the desired behavior. Starting in a quiet and familiar environment, the trainer can use a treat to guide the Pitbull into a sitting position while saying, "Sit." The instant the pit bull's hindquarters touch the ground, the trainer should click (if using clicker training) or offer verbal praise and immediately provide the treat. Consistency and repetition are vital in reinforcing the association between the command and the action, eventually leading to the Pitbull sitting in response to the verbal cue alone.

The "stay" command is essential for ensuring the Pitbull's safety and well-being in various situations. Teaching a Pitbull to stay involves building on the sit command and introducing the concept of remaining in a specific position until given further instruction. The trainer can step back and give a verbal cue, such as "stay," or use a hand signal while the Pitbull is still seated. The trainer can come back, click (if clicker training is being used), give verbal praise, and give the Pitbull a treat if it stays in its spot. The behavior is reinforced when the distance and length of stay are gradually increased. Pitbulls' comprehension of the stay command is further cemented by providing diversions and having them practice it in various settings. command. The stay command is precious when the Pitbull must remain in place, such as crossing the street or waiting at the veterinarian's office.

The recall command, "come," is a crucial element of a Pitbull's training, contributing to their safety and the owner's peace of mind. Teaching a Pitbull to come when called involves creating a positive association with the command and reinforcing the behavior with rewards. Starting in a controlled environment, the trainer can use an enthusiastic and inviting tone while saying the command "come" and rewarding the Pitbull with treats, praise, or play when they respond. Consistency is essential, and the recall command should always result in a positive experience for the Pitbull. Gradually increasing the distance and practicing in various environments helps generalize the behavior, ensuring that the Pitbull responds reliably to the recall command even in distracting situations. A reliable recall is particularly valuable for off-leash activities, allowing the owner to call the Pitbull back to their side promptly.

Training Pitbulls in basic commands establishes a foundation for obedience and strengthens the bond between the owner and the dog. Pitbulls, known for their loyalty and desire to please their owners, thrive on positive interactions and engagement. Training creates a positive and cooperative environment, fostering trust and communication between the Pitbull and their owner. During training sessions, using positive reinforcement, such as treats, praise, and play, reinforces the Pitbull's positive association with commands, creating a willing and eager learner.

Beyond the immediate benefits of obedience, basic command training contributes to the overall well-being and safety of Pitbulls. For example, the "sit" command can be instrumental in preventing jumping, which, while often fueled by excitement and affection, may be perceived as intimidating by others. Teaching the Pitbull to sit when greeting people provides a controlled and polite interaction, promoting positive experiences for the dog and those they interact with. Similarly, the "stay" command ensures the Pitbull's safety in various situations, preventing them from running into potentially dangerous areas or approaching unfamiliar dogs or people without permission.

The "come" command is vital for Pitbulls who may enjoy off-leash activities such as hiking or playing in designated areas. A reliable recall is convenient for the owner and contributes to the Pitbull's safety. The ability to call the Pitbull back promptly allows the owner to navigate potentially hazardous situations, such as encountering wildlife or approaching busy roads. A well-trained recall gives the owner confidence and peace of mind, knowing that the Pitbull will respond promptly to the command regardless of the surrounding distractions.

Training Pitbulls in basic commands also plays a significant role in challenging and dispelling negative stereotypes associated with the breed. Unfounded fears and misconceptions often contribute to breed-specific discrimination, and well-behaved and obedient Pitbulls serve as ambassadors for the breed. Public interactions that showcase a Pitbull responding positively to commands, sitting politely, staying in place, and coming when called contribute to a more positive perception of the breed within the community. Responsible ownership and positive interactions with well-trained Pitbulls help counteract stereotypes and challenge misconceptions, promoting a more inclusive view of these dogs.

It is imperative to customize the training regimen to each Pitbull's unique nature and inclinations. Although treats are a universally beneficial form of reward, certain Pitbulls may be more motivated by praise or play, while others may respond better to play. Training a Pitbull may be exciting and fun for the dog if you pay attention to how it reacts to certain things and modify your approaches accordingly. Furthermore, avoiding boredom and preserving the Pitbull's attention and passion may be achieved by mixing variation into training sessions and keeping them brief and constructive.

Consistency in training is crucial in reinforcing the desired behaviors and ensuring that the Pitbull responds reliably to commands. Training sessions should be conducted regularly, incorporating a variety of commands and gradually increasing the difficulty level. Consistency also extends to verbal cues, hand signals, and reinforcement methods, providing clarity for the Pitbull and reinforcing the association between the command and the expected behavior. Maintaining a positive and patient attitude during training sessions contributes to a positive learning experience for Pitbull.

In conclusion, basic command training is a fundamental and beneficial aspect of responsible Pitbull ownership. Teaching Pitbulls commands such as sit, stay, and come establishes essential behaviors for day-to-day living and contributes to their well-being, safety, and positive perception within the community. Training builds a foundation for obedience, fosters a strong bond between the owner and the Pitbull, and challenges negative stereotypes associated with the breed. Through positive reinforcement and consistent training, Pitbull owners can showcase their dogs' intelligence, trainability, and positive nature, contributing to a more inclusive and positive view of Pitbulls in society.

CHAPTER V

Socializing Your Pitbull

Importance of Socialization

Socialization stands as a cornerstone of responsible dog ownership, and for Pitbulls, a breed often surrounded by misconceptions, it takes on added significance. Socialization involves exposing a dog to various environments, people, animals, and stimuli in a positive and controlled manner to develop a well-adjusted and confident companion. In this section, we delve into the importance of socialization for Pitbulls, exploring how this process contributes to their overall well-being, prevents behavioral issues, and fosters positive interactions within the community.

Pitbulls, like any other breed, possess a natural curiosity and desire to explore their surroundings. However, this innate curiosity can manifest as fear or anxiety in unfamiliar situations without proper socialization. Early and positive exposure to various stimuli during the critical developmental periods of puppyhood helps shape a Pitbull's response to different environments and prevents the development of fear-based behaviors. By gradually introducing them to novel sights, sounds, smells, and experiences, owners can build the Pitbull's confidence and resilience, creating a foundation for a well-adjusted and adaptable adult dog.

A well-socialized Pitbull is more likely to exhibit appropriate behavior in different situations, reducing the risk of fear-based aggression or anxiety-driven reactions. For example, a Pitbull who has been properly socialized is less likely to react with fear or aggression when encountering new people or dogs, reducing the potential for adverse incidents. Socialization helps the Pitbull learn to navigate various social cues and interpret the intentions of others, contributing to positive interactions and preventing misunderstandings that can lead to conflicts.

Socialization is particularly crucial for Pitbulls due to the breed's history and the prevailing stereotypes associated with them. Unfounded fears and misconceptions often contribute to breed-specific legislation and discrimination against Pitbulls. Proper socialization plays a pivotal role in challenging and dispelling these stereotypes by showcasing the true nature of Pitbulls as affectionate, well-mannered, and gentle dogs. A well-socialized Pitbull serves as an ambassador for the breed, providing positive interactions with people and other animals that challenge negative perceptions and contribute to a more inclusive view of Pitbulls within the community.

Introducing a Pitbull to a diverse range of people is crucial to socialization. This includes individuals of different ages, genders, ethnicities, and appearances. Positive interactions with people from various backgrounds help Pitbull generalize their social skills, ensuring they are comfortable and well-behaved in diverse social settings. Socializing Pitbulls with children is essential, fostering a positive relationship between the dog and younger family members or visitors. Proper supervision and guidance during these interactions ensure a safe and positive experience for both the Pitbull and the children.

In addition to people, socializing Pitbulls with other dogs is essential for their overall social development. Dogs are sociable animals, and positive encounters with other dogs enhance their well-being and comprehension of social cues. Off-leash play in a controlled environment allows Pitbulls to engage in natural behaviors, develop appropriate play skills, and learn communication signals from other dogs. Well-socialized Pitbulls are likelier to exhibit friendly and non-threatening behavior during encounters with other dogs, reducing the risk of aggression or fear-based reactions.

Exposing Pitbulls to various environments is a crucial component of socialization. Different sights, sounds, and surfaces can be initially overwhelming for a dog, and gradual exposure helps them acclimate and build confidence. This includes experiences such as car rides, walks in busy urban areas, visits to parks, and exposure to different floor textures. Positive reinforcement during these experiences, such as treats, praise, and play, creates positive associations, ensuring that the Pitbull views new environments as enjoyable rather than stressful.

The importance of socialization extends beyond the puppyhood stage, as ongoing exposure to new experiences helps maintain and reinforce positive behaviors. Consistency in socialization throughout the Pitbull's life ensures they remain adaptable and comfortable in various situations. Regular outings, interactions with new people and animals, and exposure to different environments contribute to the Pitbull's continued social development and prevent regression in their behavior.

Proper socialization is especially crucial for Pitbulls who may have experienced neglect, abuse, or trauma in their past. Dogs with a history of negative experiences may be more prone to fear-based behaviors, and systematic desensitization through positive socialization helps them overcome their fears and build positive associations with new experiences. When socializing Pitbulls with a complicated past, it's essential to be patient and compassionate and to provide positive reinforcement. Gradual exposure in a safe setting can also help them regain confidence and trust.

Professional training classes and socialization groups can be valuable resources for Pitbull owners seeking guidance and support in the socialization process. These settings provide controlled environments with experienced trainers who can guide owners in the proper techniques for introducing their Pitbulls to various stimuli. Additionally, the presence of other dogs in these settings allows for positive interactions and play, contributing to the Pitbull's social skills.

Despite the benefits of socialization, there are potential challenges and risks that owners should be aware of. Over-socialization, or exposing a pit bull to too many stimuli in a short period, can be overwhelming and counterproductive. Owners should pace the socialization process and monitor the Pitbull's reactions to ensure that they remain comfortable and relaxed. Additionally, owners should prioritize the safety of their Pitbull and avoid exposing them to potentially dangerous situations or aggressive dogs during socialization.

In conclusion, the importance of socialization for Pitbulls cannot be overstated. This procedure is essential to building confidence, preventing behavioral issues, and fostering positive interactions within the community. Proper socialization contributes to the overall well-being of Pitbulls by creating well-adjusted, adaptable, and confident individuals. It challenges negative stereotypes associated with the breed by showcasing the true nature of Pitbulls as affectionate, social, and gentle dogs. Responsible Pitbull ownership involves a commitment to ongoing socialization, ensuring these dogs thrive as positive community members and ambassadors for their breed.

Introducing Your Pitbull to Other Pets

Introducing your Pitbull to other pets in the household is a crucial aspect of responsible ownership that requires careful planning, patience, and positive reinforcement. Pitbulls, often subjected to unfair stereotypes, are, in reality, capable of forming strong bonds with other animals when introduced appropriately. This essay explores the importance of a thoughtful and gradual introduction process, factors to consider when integrating a Pitbull with other pets, and strategies to ensure harmonious coexistence within the family.

First and foremost, the success of introducing a Pitbull to other pets hinges on the initial assessment of the individual animals involved. Each pet has its temperament, socialization history, and comfort level with other animals. Understanding the unique personalities of both the Pitbull and the existing pets sets the foundation for a tailored introduction plan. If the Pitbull has a history of aggression or fear towards other animals, professional guidance from a trainer or behaviorist may be beneficial to ensure a safe and positive introduction process.

Before the introduction, creating a controlled and neutral environment is imperative. This lessens the risk of early encounters and diminishes territorial tendencies. One way to establish neutral territory is to introduce all pets to a place they have never been before, like a peaceful park or a neighbor's yard. By doing this, the animals' innate need for territorial protection is lessened, and they can associate with one another without feeling threatened. One effective strategy for a successful introduction is a gradual and scent-based approach. Before any face-to-face interaction occurs, allow the pets to become familiar with each other's scents. This can be achieved by exchanging bedding or toys between the animals. Familiarizing the Pitbull with the smell of existing pets helps reduce anxiety and makes the initial meeting less stressful.

Once the pets have become acquainted with each other's scents, visual introduction through a barrier can be the next step. A baby gate or distinct cages that let the animals smell and view each other without coming into physical touch can be used for this. Thanks to this controlled visual introduction, they can read each other's reactions and body language securely. During this phase, rewards or praise serve as positive reinforcement that helps foster pleasant associations with the other animals' presence.

The actual physical introduction should occur gradually and under close supervision. Begin with short, supervised meetings, allowing the pets to interact in a controlled environment. During these initial interactions, observe their body language closely. Signs of curiosity, playfulness, or relaxed postures indicate positive interactions. On the other hand, signs of tension, raised fur, growling, or aggressive postures necessitate immediate separation, and the introduction process should be slowed down.

Reinforcing beneficial habits during the introduction phase requires consistency. Positive reinforcement— treats, praise, and affection—should be used when the pets behave calmly and amiably toward one another. This promotes positive associations and strengthens the notion that having the other animals around leads to enjoyable experiences.

It's important to recognize and respect the individual preferences of each pet. Some pets may be more friendly and accepting of a new addition, while others may be more reserved or territorial. Understanding all animals' cues and comfort levels is crucial for a successful integration process. If any signs of stress or discomfort persist, it may be necessary to consult with a professional trainer or behaviorist for additional guidance.

The introduction process is not limited to the initial meeting; it extends to the ongoing coexistence of the pets within the household. Providing separate feeding and sleeping areas for each pet helps prevent resource guarding and minimizes the potential for conflicts. Gradually increasing the time the pets spend together under supervision contributes to developing positive relationships.

The breed's natural predisposition to socialization significantly influences the success of introducing a Pitbull to other pets. Pitbulls, when adequately socialized from a young age, tend to be more adaptable and accepting of other animals. Early and positive exposure to different environments, people, and animals contributes to their overall sociability and reduces the likelihood of fear-based or aggressive behaviors.

The success of introducing a Pitbull to other pets also depends on the owner's commitment to training and supervision. Fostering a healthy connection between dogs requires consistent training and reinforcement of beneficial actions. Frequent mental and physical stimulation helps pitbulls focus their energy constructively and lessens the likelihood of getting into trouble with other animals.

It is crucial to recognize that each pet is an individual with its own set of needs and preferences. Some Pitbulls may naturally be gentler and more tolerant, making the introduction smoother. Others may require more time and patience. Similarly, existing pets may have varying reactions to introducing a new companion. Understanding and respecting the individuality of each pet contributes to a more successful integration.

The pets' age also plays a role in the introduction process. Puppies, including Pitbull puppies, are generally more adaptable and tend to form positive associations more quickly. Older dogs may have established preferences and habits, and their reactions to a new addition should be observed. Additionally, introducing a Pitbull to other pets when they are still a puppy allows for a more controlled and guided socialization process.

Positive reinforcement training techniques are invaluable during the introduction process. Rewarding positive behaviors, such as calmness, friendliness, and appropriate interactions, helps create a positive association with the presence of other pets. Treats, praise, and play serve as powerful motivators, encouraging the Pitbull to associate the company of other animals with positive experiences.

It is essential to acknowledge that, despite best efforts, not all pets may become best friends. While the goal is harmonious coexistence, realistic expectations are crucial. Some pets may prefer minimal interaction with others, and as long as they coexist peacefully and without stress, it is a successful integration. The key is to foster an environment where each pet feels secure and respected, even if they maintain a more independent relationship.

The introduction process is not a one-size-fits-all scenario, and owners should be prepared to adjust the pace based on the individual dynamics of their pets. Patience, understanding, and flexibility are paramount during the integration period. Consulting a qualified dog trainer or behaviorist can offer insightful advice and support if difficulties emerge.

In conclusion, introducing a Pitbull to other pets is a gradual process requiring careful planning and ongoing commitment. Positive reinforcement, gradual exposure, and close supervision contribute to a successful integration that fosters positive relationships among pets. Understanding each pet's unique personality and preferences, recognizing individual cues, and respecting their comfort levels are critical elements in creating a harmonious and cooperative environment within the household. When approached with patience and care, integrating a Pitbull with other pets can result in a rewarding and positive coexistence for all furry family members.

Positive Interaction with Humans

Pitbulls, often surrounded by misconceptions and stereotypes, are a breed that thrives on positive interactions with humans. These dogs are known for their loyalty, affectionate nature, and eagerness to please, making them excellent companions with the right environment and care. In this essay, we explore the importance of providing Pitbulls with positive interaction with humans, the role of responsible ownership in dispelling myths, and strategies for fostering solid bonds that showcase the true nature of these often-misunderstood dogs.

Building a solid and positive relationship between Pitbulls and humans begins with understanding the breed's unique characteristics and needs. Pitbulls are known for their intelligence, agility, and high energy levels. They are social animals that thrive on human companionship and are often eager to engage in various activities, from playtime to training sessions. Recognizing and appreciating these qualities forms the foundation for positive interaction, creating an environment where Pitbulls can express their natural behaviors and build a trusting relationship with their human companions.

Positive interaction with humans is especially crucial for Pitbulls due to the unjust stigmas and myths surrounding the breed. Misconceptions about Pitbull aggression have led to breed-specific legislation and discriminatory practices, contributing to the challenges faced by responsible Pitbull owners. Providing positive interactions with Pitbulls allows owners to challenge these myths by showcasing the breed's true nature – one of affection, playfulness, and loyalty. This positive exposure benefits Pitbull and contributes to changing public perceptions and fostering a more inclusive view of these dogs within the community.

Responsible ownership plays a central role in providing positive interaction for Pitbulls. This involves meeting the breed's physical and mental needs, ensuring a safe and stimulating environment, and investing time in training and socialization. Regular exercise is essential to channel the Pitbull's energy positively, preventing boredom and associated behavioral issues. Puzzle toys and training sessions are two forms of mental stimulation that help dogs become more intelligent and form close bonds with their owners.

Positive reinforcement training is a cornerstone of providing Pitbulls with positive interaction. This method rewards desirable behaviors with treats, praise, or play, creating positive associations with obedience and reinforcing the human-dog bond. Pitbulls respond well to positive reinforcement due to their intelligence and eagerness to please. This approach during training sessions helps build trust, encourages cooperation, and establishes a positive communication channel between the owner and the Pitbull.

Socialization is another critical component of positive interaction for Pitbulls. Early and positive exposure to various environments, people, and animals helps them develop into well-adjusted and confident individuals. Positive socialization experiences challenge stereotypes by demonstrating the breed's ability to interact calmly and positively with stimuli. This exposure builds resilience and contributes to a Pitbull's overall positive perception within the community.

Creating a positive environment for Pitbulls involves fostering a sense of security and trust. This includes providing a comfortable and designated space for the dog, offering regular routines, and ensuring that their basic needs are met. Consistent and positive interactions during feeding, grooming, and playtime contribute to the Pitbull's overall well-being and reinforce the bond between the dog and its owner.

Positive interaction also involves understanding and respecting the individual personality of each Pitbull. Like any breed, pitbulls have varying temperaments, preferences, and comfort levels. Some may be outgoing and social, while others may be more reserved or shy. Owners should observe Pitbull's cues and adjust their interactions accordingly, respecting the dog's boundaries and ensuring that positive experiences are tailored to their needs.

Establishing positive interaction with Pitbulls also involves dispelling common myths and educating the public about the breed. Myths surrounding Pitbull aggression often stem from misinformation and sensationalized media portrayals. Responsible owners play a crucial role in challenging these myths by showcasing their well-behaved and affectionate Pitbulls through positive interactions in the community. Public education, community engagement, and participating in positive activities with Pitbulls all contribute to changing perceptions and dispelling unfounded fears.

Children and Pitbulls can form strong bonds through positive interactions when supervised and guided appropriately. Pitbulls are known for their affectionate nature; many are exceptionally gentle with children. Responsible ownership includes teaching children and adults about appropriate behavior and dog interaction, emphasizing the importance of peaceful and respectful treatment. Positive experiences with children contribute to the overall positive image of Pitbulls and challenge stereotypes that suggest they are inherently dangerous around kids.

Positive interactions extend beyond the immediate family, including interactions with strangers and the community. Well-socialized and positively trained Pitbulls can be ambassadors for their breed, participating in community events, therapy work, or simply going for walks and engaging with neighbors. These positive interactions showcase the breed's true nature and contribute to changing public perceptions about Pitbulls, one positive encounter at a time.

Providing positive interaction with humans for Pitbulls also involves responsible practices such as proper leash etiquette and adherence to local regulations. Demonstrating responsible ownership in public spaces ensures the Pitbull's safety and fosters positive interactions with other community members. Respecting the concerns and comfort levels of others while showcasing the well-behaved nature of Pitbulls helps challenge stereotypes and promotes a more inclusive view of the breed.

Trust, consistency, and positive experiences build strong bonds between Pitbulls and humans. Owners who invest time in creating positive interactions through play, training, and affection develop a deep and lasting connection with their Pitbulls. Recognizing the breed's unique qualities and providing opportunities for positive expression helps fulfill their social and emotional needs, contributing to a well-rounded and contented companion.

In conclusion, providing Pitbulls with positive interaction with humans is a multifaceted and crucial aspect of responsible ownership. Positive interactions build trust, challenge stereotypes, and foster strong bonds between

Pitbulls and their owners. Responsible practices, positive reinforcement training, and public education all change perceptions about the breed and promote a more inclusive view of Pitbulls within the community. Through positive interactions, responsible ownership, and shared positive experiences, Pitbulls can continue to showcase their true nature as loving, loyal, and affectionate companions.

CHAPTER VI

Addressing Behavioral Issues

Aggression and Fear

Addressing behavioral issues in Pitbulls, particularly aggression and fear, requires a thoughtful and systematic approach, prioritizing the dog's well-being and those around them. It is essential to understand that behavioral problems can occur in any breed and are usually influenced by numerous factors, such as heredity, early experiences, and environment. Pitbulls are erroneously vilified as being naturally violent. This essay examines methods for dealing with fear and aggression in Pitbulls, highlighting the value of responsible dog ownership, constructive criticism, and expert advice in fostering a well-adjusted and obedient canine friend.

Understanding the root causes of aggression and fear in Pitbulls is a fundamental step in addressing these behavioral issues. Aggression can manifest in various forms, including fear-based aggression, territorial aggression, or aggression towards other animals. On the other hand, fear may result from past traumas, lack of socialization, or negative experiences. Identifying the specific triggers and context for the behavior is crucial for tailoring an effective intervention plan.

Responsible ownership plays a pivotal role in addressing behavioral issues in Pitbulls. Owners must commit to providing a safe, stable, and nurturing environment that meets their dogs' physical and mental needs. Regular exercise, mental stimulation, and positive interaction with humans and other animals are essential components of responsible ownership that contribute to a well-balanced and contented Pitbull.

Training based on positive reinforcement is an effective method for managing aggression and fear in Pitbulls. This approach emphasizes building trust between the dog and the owner, rewarding good behavior with toys, praise, or food, and developing positive connections with obedience. By progressively exposing the Pitbull to the feared stimuli in a controlled and pleasant manner, positive reinforcement can successfully treat fear-based aggression by rewarding calm and non-aggressive behavior.

When handling behavioral problems with Pitbulls, expert advice from a licensed dog trainer or behaviorist is priceless. These professionals can analyze the dog's behavior in detail, pinpoint stressors, and create a customized training schedule. Their expertise and experience help to create a more thorough and successful intervention by assisting owners in putting safe and efficient techniques to deal with aggressiveness and fear into practice.

Early socialization is a critical component in treating aggression in Pitbulls. A well-adjusted and socially adept adult dog results from early exposure to various people, animals, and situations throughout the crucial formative stage, which also helps reduce fear-based aggressiveness. Positive reinforcement and progressive exposure assist in fostering the development of a Pitbull's confidence and trust in various contexts. Socialization should be a joyful process.

When addressing fear in Pitbulls, it is essential to create a safe and supportive environment. Identifying and avoiding known triggers when possible helps reduce stress and anxiety in the dog. Under a professional's guidance, desensitization and counter-conditioning involve exposing the Pitbull to feared stimuli in a controlled and positive manner, gradually changing their emotional response from fear to a more positive association.

Consistency in training and clear communication with the Pitbull are critical elements in addressing behavioral issues. Establishing a set of rules and boundaries helps create a structured environment, reducing confusion and anxiety for the dog. Consistent reinforcement of desirable behaviors and immediate correction of unwanted behaviors provide clarity and contribute to a more positive and cooperative relationship.

It is important to note that punishment-based training methods are not recommended for addressing aggression or fear in Pitbulls. Punishment can make people feel more afraid and anxious, making them react defensively or aggressively. Positive reinforcement builds a stronger, more trusting bond between the Pitbull and its owner by rewarding desired behavior.

Addressing aggression in Pitbulls also involves understanding the specific triggers and contexts that elicit aggressive behavior. Aggression can be directed towards strangers, animals, or even family members. Identifying the situations that provoke aggression allows for targeted training and management strategies. For example, if a Pitbull exhibits aggression towards strangers, gradual exposure to new people in a controlled setting, combined with positive reinforcement, can help modify their behavior.

Creating a consistent routine and providing mental stimulation are essential components of addressing behavioral issues in Pitbulls. Puzzle feeders, interactive toys, and mentally demanding activities all help to create a more balanced and pleased dog.

The Pitbull's health may also influence behavioral problems. A physical hurt or discomfort can show up as fear or aggressiveness. Routine veterinary examinations are crucial to rule out any underlying medical conditions causing behavioral concerns. Resolving the dog's physical discomfort can significantly affect its behavior and general well-being.

When addressing fear in Pitbulls, it is essential to avoid reinforcing anxious behavior inadvertently. Comforting or coddling a fearful Pitbull may inadvertently reinforce the fear response. Instead, remaining calm and providing positive reinforcement for calm behavior helps shift the Pitbull's emotional response to a more positive one. Gradual exposure to the feared stimuli in a controlled and positive manner helps desensitize the dog over time. Creating a safe space or designated area for the Pitbull can be beneficial in addressing fear-based behaviors. This area serves as a retreat where the Pitbull can feel secure and calm. Positive experiences in this safe space contribute to the dog's overall sense of security and help reduce fear-based behaviors.

Owners must educate themselves about canine body language and communication to better understand their Pitbull's signals. Recognizing signs of stress, anxiety, or fear allows owners to intervene appropriately and adjust their approach to ensure a positive interaction. A relaxed and confident owner contributes to a more secure and well-behaved Pitbull.

In conclusion, addressing behavioral issues such as aggression and fear in Pitbulls requires a comprehensive and compassionate approach. Responsible ownership, positive reinforcement training, early socialization, and professional guidance are vital in promoting a well-balanced and contented Pitbull. By understanding each dog's individual needs and triggers and tailoring interventions accordingly, owners can build trust, dispel myths, and foster strong bonds with their Pitbulls, showcasing the breed's true nature as loyal, affectionate, and resilient companions.

Separation Anxiety

Separation anxiety, a common behavioral issue in dogs, can be a challenging concern for Pitbull owners. Pitbulls, known for their loyalty and affectionate nature, may develop separation anxiety when left alone, leading to distressing behaviors such as excessive barking, destructive chewing, and attempts to escape. In this section, we explore a comprehensive approach to addressing separation anxiety in Pitbulls, encompassing understanding the root causes, implementing positive training techniques, creating a supportive environment, and seeking professional guidance to ensure the dog's and the owner's well-being.

Pitbulls, as a breed known for forming strong bonds with their owners, may be particularly prone to separation anxiety. Factors such as changes in routine, a history of abandonment or rehoming, or even a traumatic event during the owner's absence can contribute to the development of separation anxiety. Identifying the specific triggers and context for the anxiety allows owners to tailor their approach to address the underlying causes.

Positive reinforcement training is a cornerstone of addressing separation anxiety in Pitbulls. This method focuses on rewarding desirable behaviors with treats, praise, or play, creating positive associations with being alone, and reinforcing the bond between the dog and the owner. Gradual desensitization to being alone, starting with short periods and gradually increasing the duration, allows the Pitbull to acclimate to the experience positively. Positive reinforcement during departures and arrivals helps create positive associations with the owner's comings and goings, reducing anxiety.

Creating a supportive environment is essential in addressing separation anxiety. Providing engaging toys, puzzle feeders, or treat-dispensing toys can keep the Pitbull mentally stimulated during periods of alone time. A designated and comfortable space, such as a cozy bed or crate, can serve as a safe retreat for the Pitbull, contributing to their overall sense of security. Additionally, leaving items with the owner's scent, such as clothing, can provide comfort in their absence.

Consistency in routines and departures is crucial for managing separation anxiety in Pitbulls. Establishing a predictable routine helps the dog anticipate periods of alone time, reducing anxiety associated with departures. Varying departure cues, such as picking up keys or putting on shoes, during non-departure times help desensitize the Pitbull to these triggers and minimize anxiety. Consistency in departure and arrival routines contributes to a sense of predictability for the Pitbull.

Gradual desensitization to departures is a critical element in addressing separation anxiety. This involves exposing the Pitbull to cues associated with departures in a controlled and positive manner without actually leaving. For example, picking up keys or putting on a coat can be related to positive experiences, such as play or treats, to change the emotional response of the Pitbull to these cues. This process helps the dog form positive associations with departure-related stimuli.

Professional guidance is invaluable when addressing separation anxiety in Pitbulls. A certified dog trainer or behaviorist can thoroughly assess the dog's behavior, identify triggers, and develop a tailored training plan. Their expertise allows for a more comprehensive and effective intervention, guiding owners in implementing strategies to address separation anxiety safely and effectively. A veterinarian should also be consulted to rule out potential medical diseases causing the behavioral issues.

Addressing separation anxiety also involves refraining from punishment-based methods. Punishment can exacerbate anxiety and fear, leading to defensive or aggressive responses. Positive reinforcement training rewards the desired behavior, creating a more positive and trusting relationship between the Pitbull and the owner. Punishment can erode trust and worsen anxiety, hindering the progress of addressing separation anxiety.

Implementing a systematic departure routine helps ease the transition for the Pitbull. This involves gradually increasing the duration of departures in a controlled manner, starting with short intervals and gradually extending the time. Positive reinforcement during departures and rewards for calm behavior upon return contribute to a positive association with being alone. This approach helps the Pitbull learn that departures are not permanent and are followed by the owner's return.

Counter-conditioning is a technique that can be used to change the emotional response of the Pitbull to being alone. This involves associating being alone with positive experiences, such as receiving treats or engaging in enjoyable activities. Gradually increasing the duration of alone time while providing positive reinforcement helps the Pitbull form positive associations with being by themselves, reducing anxiety.

Interactive toys and mental stimulation are essential components of managing separation anxiety. Providing toys that dispense treats or engage the Pitbull mentally can distract them and alleviate boredom during alone time. Puzzle feeders or frozen stuffed Kongs can be particularly effective in keeping the dog occupied and providing a positive association with being alone.

Creating a consistent departure cue can help signal to the Pitbull that the owner will return. This can be a specific phrase or action consistently associated with departures. Using this cue during departures and pairing it with positive reinforcement can help the Pitbull understand that the owner will return, reducing anxiety associated with being alone.

Using calming products or pheromone diffusers may be beneficial in some cases. Calming products, such as anxiety wraps or calming collars, can provide a sense of security for the Pitbull. Pheromone diffusers release synthetic pheromones that mimic the calming scents produced by nursing mother dogs, contributing to a relaxed environment. While these products may not work for every dog, some owners find them helpful in managing separation anxiety.

When treating separation anxiety, it is essential to maintain consistency and patience. There's a chance for setbacks and steady progress. A calm and happy attitude during arrivals and departures and the celebration of tiny achievements help create a welcoming and understanding atmosphere for the Pitbull. Long-term success depends on maintaining consistency in management and training techniques.

In conclusion, treating separation anxiety in pit bulls necessitates a kind and diverse strategy. A thorough intervention approach includes identifying the underlying problems, implementing positive reinforcement, fostering a supportive environment, and getting expert advice. Through customization of tactics to suit each Pitbull's unique requirements and regular reinforcement of good behavior, owners may assist their dogs in overcoming separation anxiety and create a more harmonious and pleased canine friend.

Excessive Barking and Digging

In dogs, especially Pitbulls, behavioral problems, including excessive barking and digging, are not uncommon. Although these actions can typically manifest a dog's instincts, they may become troublesome if they happen frequently or in the wrong situations. This essay examines doable tactics for dealing with Pitbulls' excessive barking and digging, highlighting the significance of comprehending the underlying causes, using positive training techniques, offering mental and physical stimulation, and establishing a supportive environment to promote balanced canine companions.

Creating a successful intervention strategy requires understanding the underlying reasons for excessive digging and barking. Pitbulls may exhibit these behaviors for various reasons, given their intelligence and intense energy levels. A dog may bark to communicate, to pass the time, to attract attention, or to show fear or boredom. Digging, however, can sometimes be an instinctive behavior, such as finding a cozy place to relax or investigating smells in the ground. Owners can adjust their strategy to address the root causes of these behaviors by pinpointing the precise triggers and situations that set them off.

Positive reinforcement training is powerful in modifying behavioral issues such as excessive barking and digging in Pitbulls. This approach focuses on rewarding desirable behaviors with treats, praise, or play, creating positive associations, and reinforcing the bond between the dog and the owner. Teaching a "quiet" command and rewarding silence with positive reinforcement can be effective for excessive barking. For digging, redirecting the behavior towards a designated digging area and rewarding the dog for using that space can help modify the behavior positively.

Treating behavioral problems in Pitbulls requires both mental and physical stimulation. Excessive digging and barking are two ways that bored and overactive energy can release stored energy. The Pitbull's energy may be constructively channeled, and these undesirable behaviors can be avoided with regular exercise, interactive play, and exciting hobbies like puzzle toys or obedience training sessions. In particular, mental stimulation is sometimes overlooked but makes a big difference in a dog's ability to live in balance and be happy.

Creating a conducive environment involves setting the Pitbull up for success and minimizing excessive barking and digging opportunities. For barking, reducing exposure to stimuli that trigger excessive vocalization, such as people passing by or other animals, can help manage the behavior. Providing a designated digging area with loose soil or sand allows the Pitbull to express this natural behavior appropriately. Consistency in managing the environment contributes to long-term success.

Understanding the individual triggers for excessive barking is critical to addressing the behavior effectively. If the Pitbull barks excessively due to boredom, providing toys, puzzle feeders, or rotating play items can keep them mentally stimulated. If barking is attention-seeking, teaching the dog alternative behaviors, such as sitting quietly and rewarding this behavior with attention, helps shift the focus positively. Identifying and addressing the specific cause allows for a more targeted intervention. For

excessive digging, understanding the motivation behind the behavior is essential. Providing shaded areas or cooling mats can address the underlying need if the Pitbull digs to create an excellent resting spot. If digging results from curiosity or exploration, incorporating interactive toys or scent-based activities can redirect the behavior positively. Identifying the motivation for digging allows owners to address the root cause effectively.

Getting expert advice from a behaviorist or qualified dog trainer can be quite helpful for managing excessive digging and barking. These professionals can analyze the dog's behavior in detail, pinpoint stressors, and create a customized training schedule. Their expertise and experience help make a more thorough and successful intervention by assisting owners in putting these behaviors into practice safely and efficiently. Getting professional assistance also aids in ruling out any medical conditions that might be causing behavioral concerns. Consistency in training is crucial for modifying behavioral issues in Pitbulls. Whether addressing excessive barking or digging, owners must consistently respond to undesirable behaviors and reinforce positive alternatives. Inconsistency can confuse the Pitbull and hinder the effectiveness of behavior modification efforts. Establishing clear expectations and always supporting desired behaviors contribute to successful behavior modification.

When addressing excessive barking, it is essential to identify the different types of barking and tailor the intervention accordingly. Alarm barking in response to perceived threats, boredom barking, attention-seeking barking, or play barking may require different approaches. Understanding the context and motivation behind each type of barking allows for a more targeted and effective intervention. Positive reinforcement for quiet behavior, providing alternative activities, or addressing the underlying cause, such as boredom, can be part of the strategy.

Providing a designated area for excessive digging allows the Pitbull to express this natural behavior appropriately. The digging area can be filled with loose soil or sand, and burying toys or treats in this space can make it more enticing for the dog. Consistent positive reinforcement for using the designated area and redirecting the behavior when digging elsewhere contribute to modifying this behavior positively.

It is essential to avoid punishment-based methods when addressing excessive barking and digging. Punishment can lead to fear and anxiety, exacerbating behavioral issues and potentially causing new problems. Positive reinforcement training focuses on rewarding desirable behaviors, creating positive associations, and reinforcing the dog's and the owner's bond. Punishment-based methods can damage the trust between the Pitbull and the owner, hindering the progress of behavior modification.

Creating a routine incorporating mental and physical exercise helps prevent excessive barking and digging. Regular walks, play sessions, and training activities mentally and physically engage the Pitbull, reducing boredom and excess energy. Providing a structured routine contributes to a sense of predictability and helps minimize opportunities for undesirable behaviors. Consistency in routine and positive reinforcement for appropriate behaviors contribute to long-term success.

Environmental enrichment is one of the most important strategies for treating behavioral problems in Pitbulls. Various toys, puzzle feeders, and engaging activities help prevent boredom and keep the Pitbull cognitively busy. Switch up the toys and add new activities regularly to avoid boredom and stimulate your dog's curiosity. Enrichment, both mentally and physically, makes a Pitbull happier and more balanced, which reduces the chance of overzealous digging and barking.

It's critical to distinguish between alert barking—which alerts its owner to possible threats—and bored or attention-seeking barking when dealing with excessive barking. If the barking is from boredom, offering puzzle feeders, engaging toys, or switching up play activities can help refocus the behavior constructively. Teaching the dog, a "quiet" command and rewarding calm behavior can assist in changing the behavior if the barking is alert-based.

Getting routine veterinary examinations to rule out any probable medical conditions causing excessive digging or barking is critical. Behavior can be influenced by pain, discomfort, or underlying medical illnesses; therefore, treating these problems may be essential to changing behavior. A vet can evaluate the dog's general health and provide direction for any required medical procedures.

In conclusion, addressing excessive barking and digging in Pitbulls requires a comprehensive and tailored approach that considers the individual needs and motivations of the dog. Understanding the root causes, employing positive reinforcement training, providing mental and physical stimulation, creating a conducive environment, and seeking professional guidance contribute to a successful behavior modification plan. Through consistent and compassionate interventions, owners can foster well-balanced and contented Pitbulls, showcasing the breed's true nature as intelligent, energetic, and loyal companions.

CHAPTER VII

Physical and Mental Exercise

Daily Exercise Requirements

Pitbulls, known for their strength, agility, and boundless energy, are a breed that thrives on regular physical and mental health maintenance through exercise. Understanding and meeting the daily exercise requirements of a pit bull is essential for fostering a healthy and contented canine companion. In this essay, we explore the importance of exercise for Pitbulls, factors influencing their activity needs, and practical strategies for ensuring they receive adequate physical and mental stimulation.

Pitbulls, like many other dog breeds, are descendants of working and hunting dogs. Historically bred for tasks such as bull-baiting and later as farm dogs, they possess a natural athleticism and vigor. While modern Pitbulls may not be engaged in the same historical tasks, their innate traits make them a high-energy breed that benefits significantly from regular exercise.

Several factors, including age, health, and individual temperament, influence the daily exercise requirements for a Pitbull. Puppies, in particular, require a structured exercise routine to burn off excess energy and promote healthy growth. Young Pitbulls may be more exuberant and playful, necessitating frequent play sessions and short walks. Adult Pitbulls generally thrive on more extended and vigorous activities, while senior dogs may have lower energy levels and benefit from gentler exercises.

A crucial aspect of addressing the daily exercise needs of a Pitbull is understanding the breed's predisposition to certain behaviors. Pitbulls, being intelligent and social dogs, require mental stimulation and physical activity. Therefore, incorporating activities that engage their minds, such as puzzle toys, obedience training, or interactive play, is essential for a well-rounded exercise regimen.

Regular walks are a fundamental component of a Pitbull's daily exercise routine. These walks provide an opportunity for physical exercise, mental stimulation, and socialization. Pitbulls, being social animals, benefit from exposure to different environments, people, and other dogs. While individual exercise needs may vary, a general guideline is to aim for at least 30 to 60 minutes of daily walks. This helps burn off energy and strengthens the bond between the Pitbull and its owner.

Beyond walks, engaging in more active and dynamic exercises is vital for meeting the Pitbull's exercise requirements. Play sessions in secure, fenced areas allow them to run, jump, and exhibit natural athleticism. Games of fetch or tug-of-war can be excellent outlets for their energy. For Pitbulls that enjoy swimming, water activities provide a low-impact and enjoyable form of exercise. Incorporating various activities prevents monotony and ensures the dog remains mentally and physically stimulated.

Interactive toys and puzzle feeders are valuable tools in meeting the mental stimulation needs of Pitbulls. Consideration should be given to the durability of toys, as Pitbulls are strong chewers. Toys that dispense treats or can be filled with food engage the dog's mind and encourage focused play, preventing boredom-related behaviors.

Obedience training serves a dual purpose for Pitbulls – it provides mental stimulation and reinforces positive behavior. These intelligent dogs enjoy learning new commands and tricks. Regular training sessions exercise their minds and contribute to a well-behaved and responsive companion. Positive reinforcement techniques, using treats or praise, enhance the training experience and strengthen the bond between the Pitbull and its owner.

Incorporating off-leash activities in safe and enclosed environments allows Pitbulls to experience greater freedom and independence. Dog parks or securely fenced areas provide supervised play with other dogs, promoting socialization and mental engagement. Off-leash activities should be introduced gradually and controlled, ensuring the Pitbull's recall responsiveness and compatibility with other dogs.

Running or jogging alongside a biking owner is another effective way to meet the Pitbull's exercise needs. This activity provides physical and mental stimulation, allowing the dog to keep pace with its owner's energy levels. However, it is crucial to ensure the safety and well-being of the Pitbull during such activities by using proper equipment, starting with shorter distances, and being attentive to signs of fatigue or discomfort.

Agility training is an excellent option for Pitbulls that enjoy a more structured and challenging form of exercise. Agility courses engage the dog's body and mind with obstacles such as tunnels, jumps, and weave poles. Participating in agility activities meets their exercise requirements and hones their agility, coordination, and responsiveness to commands. Many Pitbulls find agility training to be a rewarding and enjoyable experience.

Pitbulls must get the recommended amount of activity each day, but it's just as essential to adjust the time and intensity of activities to suit the needs of each dog. It is necessary to consider factors including age, health, and previous medical issues. For example, older dogs and puppies may tolerate different food or energy levels. When creating an exercise regimen for Pitbull, owners should speak with their veterinarian about what suits their needs.

One challenge Pitbull owners may encounter is weather-related restrictions on outdoor activities. Extreme heat, cold, or inclement weather can limit the duration and intensity of exercise. During such conditions, indoor activities, such as interactive play, obedience training, or indoor fetch, become essential to maintain the Pitbull's physical and mental well-being. Additionally, considering alternative forms of exercise, such as treadmill training or indoor agility courses, helps ensure a consistent exercise routine regardless of outdoor conditions.

While meeting the daily exercise requirements for a Pitbull is crucial, it is equally essential to be mindful of their comfort and safety during activities. Adequate hydration, especially during warm weather, is necessary to prevent dehydration. Checking for signs of fatigue, such as excessive panting or slowing down, allows owners to adjust the intensity and duration of exercise accordingly. Providing shaded areas and avoiding exercise during the hottest parts of the day contribute to the Pitbull's well-being.

Socialization is an integral component of a Pitbull's exercise routine. These dogs, often unfairly stigmatized, benefit greatly from positive interactions with other dogs and people. Dog-friendly parks, group walks, or organized playdates offer opportunities for Pitbulls to socialize, fostering positive behavior and preventing aggression or fear-related issues. Early and ongoing socialization contributes to a well-adjusted and confident Pitbull.

In conclusion, meeting the daily exercise requirements for a Pitbull is essential for promoting their physical and mental well-being. Regular walks, active play sessions, interactive toys, obedience training, and various activities contribute to a well-rounded exercise routine. Tailoring the intensity and duration of activities to the individual dog's needs, considering factors such as age and health, ensures a balanced approach to exercise. Socialization and mental stimulation are equally crucial components of a Pitbull's daily routine, fostering a healthy, contented, well-behaved canine companion. Responsible and attentive ownership and commitment to meeting these exercise needs allow Pitbulls to showcase their true nature as loyal, intelligent, and energetic companions.

Enrichment Activities

Pitbulls, known for their strength, intelligence, and boundless energy, are a breed that thrives on various enrichment activities to maintain both physical and mental well-being. Enrichment goes beyond mere exercise, encompassing activities that stimulate a pit bull's mind, engage its senses, and fulfill its natural instincts. This section delves into the significance of enrichment for Pitbulls, examines the vast array of activities that meet their specific requirements, and discusses how responsible ownership can result in a happy and well-rounded dog friend.

Enrichment activities play a crucial role in enhancing Pitbulls' overall quality of life. These activities go beyond the physical aspect of exercise and address the breed's intelligence, curiosity, and need for mental stimulation. Pitbulls, being intelligent and social dogs, benefit significantly from activities that engage their minds, prevent boredom-related behaviors, and foster a more balanced and contented life. Enrichment is not merely a luxury for these dogs; it is a fundamental aspect of responsible ownership that contributes to their well-being.

One fundamental form of enrichment for Pitbulls is interactive play with toys. Pitbulls, strong chewers, benefit from durable toys that can withstand their powerful jaws. Toys that dispense treats or have different textures engage their senses and provide mental stimulation. Interactive play fulfills their need for physical activity and strengthens the bond between the Pitbull and its owner. It is essential to rotate toys regularly to keep the activities novel and prevent monotony.

Puzzle toys are excellent tools for mental enrichment. These toys challenge the Pitbull's problem-solving skills as they discover how to access treats or kibble hidden within. Puzzle feeders, treat-dispensing balls, and other interactive toys make mealtime more engaging, turning a routine activity into a mentally stimulating experience. Incorporating a variety of puzzle toys prevents boredom and gives the Pitbull a sense of accomplishment.

Obedience training serves as both mental and physical enrichment for Pitbulls. These intelligent dogs enjoy learning new commands and tricks, and regular training sessions exercise their minds and contribute to a well-behaved and responsive companion. Positive reinforcement techniques, using treats or praise, enhance the training experience and strengthen the bond between the Pitbull and its owner. Obedience training also provides an avenue for socialization, teaching the dog to respond to commands in various environments and around different people.

Sensory enrichment is another vital aspect of a Pitbull's well-rounded life. Engaging their senses through activities such as sniffing, exploring new textures, or experiencing different environments contributes to their mental stimulation. Taking the Pitbull on different walking routes, allowing them to investigate various scents, or providing opportunities for exploration in safe and controlled settings enhances their sensory experiences. Sensory enrichment is particularly beneficial for these dogs, as their strong sense of smell and curiosity are intrinsic characteristics.

One often underestimated form of enrichment for Pitbulls is socialization. Despite their sometimes-unfair reputation, Pitbulls are social animals that benefit greatly from positive interactions with other dogs and people. Organized playdates, visits to dog-friendly parks, or joining group walks provide opportunities for the Pitbull to socialize, fostering positive behavior and preventing fear or aggression-related issues. Early and ongoing socialization contributes to a well-adjusted and confident Pitbull.

Physical activities beyond routine walks further contribute to a Pitbull's overall enrichment. Activities such as agility training provide both mental and physical stimulation. Agility courses engage the dog's body and mind with obstacles such as tunnels, jumps, and weave poles. Participating in agility activities meets their exercise requirements and hones their agility, coordination, and responsiveness to commands. Many Pitbulls find agility training to be a rewarding and enjoyable experience.

Water activities like swimming offer low-impact exercise and enrichment for Pitbulls. Not only does swimming provide a full-body workout, but it also offers a unique sensory experience. Introducing Pitbulls to water gradually and ensuring a positive association with swimming can turn this activity into enjoyable enrichment. Swimming is particularly beneficial for Pitbulls with joint or mobility issues, providing a less strenuous but effective exercise option.

Creating opportunities for problem-solving is an integral aspect of mental enrichment. Pitbulls, being intelligent dogs, enjoy activities that challenge their cognitive abilities. Hide-and-seek games with treats, where the Pitbull has to find hidden snacks in the house or yard, engage their sense of smell, and provide mental stimulation. Interactive food puzzles that require the dog to figure out how to access treats stimulate problem-solving skills and keep the mind active.

Chew toys serve a dual purpose for Pitbulls – they provide mental enrichment and an outlet for their natural chewing instincts. Choosing durable and safe chew toys is crucial, considering the strength of a Pitbull's jaws. Chewing keeps them occupied and promotes dental health by reducing plaque and tartar buildup. Incorporating a variety of chew toys, such as rubber toys, nylon bones, or dental chews, prevents boredom and satisfies their need to chew positively.

Creating a safe and comfortable space for the Pitbull also contributes to their enrichment. This space is a calming environment where the Pitbull can relax and feel safe. Positive experiences in their designated space contribute to their overall sense of well-being.

Consideration should be given to the Pitbull's individual preferences and temperament when selecting enrichment activities. While some Pitbulls may enjoy more active and dynamic activities, others prefer gentler mental stimulation. Paying attention to the dog's reactions and tailoring activities to their preferences ensures the enrichment experience is enjoyable and beneficial. Flexibility in incorporating various activities prevents routine and keeps the Pitbull engaged.

Responsible ownership is a crucial component of providing adequate enrichment for Pitbulls. Understanding the breed's characteristics, recognizing individual needs, and dedicating time and effort to their well-being contribute to a happy and contented canine companion. Regular veterinary check-ups ensure that the Pitbull is in good health, allowing owners to tailor enrichment activities based on specific medical considerations. Responsible ownership also involves monitoring the Pitbull's reactions during activities, ensuring their safety and well-being.

Despite their sometimes-unwarranted negative reputation, Pitbulls are affectionate, loyal, and highly trainable dogs that can thrive in enriched environments. Responsible ownership, incorporating various activities that cater to their physical and mental needs, promotes their overall well-being, and challenges misperceptions about the breed. Enrichment activities are not just a luxury for Pitbulls; they are a fundamental aspect of providing a fulfilling and contented life for this intelligent and loving companion.

Stimulating Your Pitbull's Mind

Pitbulls, renowned for their strength, loyalty, and boundless energy, are intelligent and curious dogs that thrive on mental stimulation. While physical exercise is essential for their well-being, stimulating their minds is equally crucial for a balanced and contented life. In this section, we explore the importance of mental stimulation for Pitbulls, delve into the breed's cognitive capabilities, and discuss various activities that cater to their intellectual needs. Understanding how to engage and challenge a Pitbull's mind contributes to their overall happiness and strengthens the bond between the dog and its owner.

Pitbulls, like many other intelligent breeds, benefit significantly from mental stimulation. While their physical prowess often takes center stage, neglecting their cognitive needs can lead to boredom-related behaviors, such as chewing, digging, or excessive barking. Engaging a Pitbull's mind prevents undesirable behaviors and provides an outlet for their innate intelligence and curiosity. Mental stimulation contributes to a well-rounded and contented Pitbull, showcasing the breed's true nature beyond its muscular physique.

Understanding Pitbulls' cognitive capabilities is essential for tailoring practical mental stimulation activities. Pitbulls enjoy challenges that require them to think and use their senses. Whether figuring out how to access treats hidden in a puzzle toy or mastering a new trick during training, Pitbulls thrive on activities that engage their minds and tap into their natural intelligence.

Interactive play with toys is a fundamental way to stimulate a pit bull's mind. Durable toys that dispense treats or have different textures engage their senses and provide mental stimulation. Interactive play fulfills their need for physical activity and challenges their problem-solving skills. Toys that encourage the Pitbull to work for rewards, such as treat-dispensing balls or puzzle feeders, turn playtime into a mentally enriching experience. Regularly rotating toys keep the activities novel and prevent boredom.

Obedience training is a powerful tool for stimulating a Pitbull's mind and fostering a stronger bond between the dog and its owner. These intelligent dogs enjoy learning new commands and tricks, and regular training sessions exercise their minds and contribute to a well-behaved and responsive companion. Positive reinforcement techniques, using treats or praise, enhance the training experience and create a positive association with learning. Teaching Pitbull new tricks or reinforcing existing commands keeps their minds sharp and engaged.

Sensory enrichment is another vital aspect of stimulating a Pitbull's mind. Engaging their senses through activities such as sniffing, exploring new textures, or experiencing different environments contributes to their mental well-being. Pitbulls have a keen sense of smell, and providing opportunities for scent-based activities, such as hiding treats around the house or yard, taps into their instincts. Regular walks in different environments expose them to new sights, sounds, and smells, enriching their sensory experiences.

Problem-solving activities, such as hide-and-seek games, provide mental stimulation for Pitbulls. Creating scavenger hunts or using interactive toys that require the dog to manipulate parts to access treats fosters problem-solving skills. These activities provide mental stimulation and keep the Pitbull entertained and focused.

Chew toys serve a dual purpose for Pitbulls – they provide mental enrichment and an outlet for their natural chewing instincts. Choosing durable and safe chew toys is crucial, considering the strength of a Pitbull's jaws. Chewing keeps them occupied and promotes dental health by reducing plaque and tartar buildup. Incorporating a variety of chew toys, such as rubber toys, nylon bones, or dental chews, prevents boredom and satisfies their need to chew positively.

Interactive food puzzles are practical tools for mental stimulation. These puzzles require the Pitbull to manipulate parts or solve challenges to access treats or kibble. Food puzzles come in various designs, from simple ones that need rolling to more complex ones that involve sliding or rotating parts. Using interactive puzzles during mealtime turns a routine activity into a mentally engaging experience. It also slows down the pace of eating, promoting better digestion.

Engaging in nose work activities taps into the Pitbull's strong sense of smell and provides mental stimulation. Nose work involves teaching the dog to find hidden scents or objects using their sense of smell. Introducing them to new scents or creating scent trails for them to follow adds a layer of complexity, making nose work an enriching and engaging activity.

Interactive play with the owner, such as fetch or tug-of-war, provides physical exercise and stimulates the Pitbull's mind. Incorporating variations, such as hiding toys or changing the game's rules, keeps the activity exciting and mentally enriching. Playing with the owner strengthens the bond between the Pitbull and its family, creating a positive and interactive relationship. It also allows the owner to observe and understand the dog's behaviors and preferences.

Agility courses engage the dog's body and mind with obstacles such as tunnels, jumps, and weave poles. Participating in agility activities meets their exercise requirements and hones their agility, coordination, and responsiveness to commands. Many Pitbulls find agility training to be a rewarding and enjoyable experience, combining physical activity with mental challenges.

Creating a stimulating environment at home contributes to a Pitbull's mental well-being. Creating designated play areas or incorporating climbing structures and tunnels complicates their environment. A comfortable and safe space with a mix of toys, chew items, and interactive puzzles ensures that the Pitbull has opportunities for mental stimulation even when the owner is not actively involved.

Responsible ownership plays a crucial role in effectively stimulating a Pitbull's mind. Understanding the breed's characteristics, recognizing individual needs, and dedicating time and effort to their well-being contribute to a happy and contented canine companion. Regular veterinary check-ups ensure that the Pitbull is in good health, allowing owners to tailor mental stimulation activities based on specific medical considerations. Responsible ownership also involves monitoring the Pitbull's reactions during activities, ensuring their safety and well-being.

In conclusion, stimulating a Pitbull's mind is an integral aspect of responsible ownership that contributes to their well-being. Engaging their intelligence and curiosity through interactive play, obedience training, sensory enrichment, problem-solving activities, and various interactive toys fosters a more balanced and contented life. Responsible owners who invest time and effort in understanding their Pitbull's individual preferences and providing a stimulating environment prevent behavioral issues and create a strong and positive bond with their intelligent and loving companions.

CHAPTER VIII

Health and Nutrition

Regular Vet Check-ups

Regular veterinary check-ups are a cornerstone of responsible pet ownership. For Pitbulls, a breed known for its strength, loyalty, and affectionate nature, these check-ups are crucial for maintaining their overall health and well-being. In this section, we explore the importance of routine veterinary care for Pitbulls, discuss the specific health considerations associated with the breed, and emphasize the role of preventive healthcare in ensuring a long and healthy life for these beloved canine companions.

Pitbulls, like all dog breeds, benefit significantly from regular veterinary check-ups. While Pitbulls are often associated with resilience and robustness, they are not immune to health issues, and early detection and intervention through regular vet check-ups can make a significant difference in their overall quality of life.

One primary aspect of regular veterinary check-ups for Pitbulls involves preventive care measures. Preventative care is designed to identify and address potential health issues before they escalate, contributing to a healthier and longer life for the dog. This includes routine vaccinations to protect against common canine diseases, regular parasite control to prevent infestations, and dental care to maintain oral health. Pitbulls, known for their powerful jaws, may benefit from dental check-ups and cleanings to prevent dental issues that can impact their overall well-being.

Nutritional guidance is another crucial component of regular vet check-ups for Pitbulls. The breed's muscular build and energetic nature necessitate a well-balanced and appropriate diet to support their overall health. Regular weight monitoring and nutritional assessments help ensure Pitbulls receive the necessary nutrients. Veterinarians can provide tailored advice on feeding schedules, portion sizes, and dietary choices to maintain a healthy weight and prevent obesity-related issues, which can be a concern for this breed.

Regular vet check-ups are an opportune time to address behavioral or psychological concerns that may affect Pitbulls. These dogs are known for their intelligence and loyalty but may also exhibit certain behaviors requiring attention. Additionally, routine vet visits provide an avenue for discussing training strategies and mental stimulation activities and addressing concerns about the Pitbull's overall well-being.

Preventive care for Pitbulls also includes screenings for breed-specific health considerations. While Pitbulls are generally a healthy breed, they may be predisposed to certain conditions, such as hip dysplasia or allergies. Frequent veterinary examinations facilitate the early identification of these problems through screens, allowing veterinarians and their owners to create management or intervention plans. Proactive care coupled with early discovery can significantly enhance the dog's quality of life and lessen the effects of specific health issues.

For Pitbulls, vaccinations are an essential part of preventive treatment. Frequent veterinary examinations offer the chance to confirm that the dog has received all necessary immunizations. Adenovirus, distemper, parvovirus, and rabies are core immunizations shielding Pitbulls from potentially fatal illnesses. In addition, non-core vaccinations could be advised in light of the dog's lifestyle and possible exposure to particular dangers.

Parasite prevention is an essential component of routine veterinary care for Pitbulls. Fleas, ticks, and intestinal parasites can pose significant health risks to these dogs. Regular vet check-ups allow administering preventive medications to protect Pitbulls from these parasites. Preventive measures contribute to the dog's well-being and safeguard the owners and their families from potential zoonotic diseases. Veterinary guidance on effective parasite control strategies is crucial for maintaining Pitbulls' healthy and comfortable living environment.

Oral hygiene is frequently neglected regarding a Pitbull's general health, but routine veterinary exams offer an opportunity to discuss it. Pitbulls may be more susceptible to dental conditions such as gingivitis, periodontal disease, and plaque and tartar accumulation because of their powerful jaws. Veterinarians are qualified to evaluate the dog's oral health, suggest suitable dental hygiene practices, and, if required, provide professional cleanings. Maintaining good dental hygiene benefits Pitbulls' general health and supports solid teeth and gums.

As Pitbulls age, regular vet check-ups become even more critical to address age-related health considerations. Senior Pitbulls may experience changes in mobility, joint health, and organ function. Periodic monitoring through veterinary examinations, blood work, and diagnostic tests allows for early detection of age-related conditions, such as arthritis or kidney disease. Tailored healthcare plans, including dietary adjustments and lifestyle modifications, can be implemented to ensure the comfort and well-being of senior Pitbulls.

Regular vet check-ups also offer an opportunity to discuss and implement an appropriate vaccination schedule for Pitbull puppies. With their developing immune systems, puppies require a series of vaccinations to provide immunity against common diseases. Veterinarians can guide owners on the timing and types of vaccinations needed and provide advice on socialization, training, and nutrition for the growing Pitbull puppy. Early veterinary care sets the foundation for a healthy and well-adjusted adult Pitbull.

Behavioral concerns, anxiety, or changes in temperament may be indicative of underlying health issues or psychological distress. Veterinarians can guide behavior modification techniques and training strategies and, if necessary, recommend consultations with animal behaviorists. Addressing mental well-being is integral to ensuring a Pitbull's overall happiness and harmony within the family.

Responsible ownership includes understanding the specific health considerations associated with Pitbulls and actively participating in their preventive healthcare. Regular vet check-ups should be viewed as proactive rather than reactive responses to health issues. This approach allows for early intervention, preventative care, and the establishment of a strong partnership between owners and veterinarians in promoting the health and well-being of Pitbulls.

While regular vet check-ups are essential, it is equally crucial for owners to be observant of any changes in their Pitbull's behavior, appetite, or physical condition between appointments. Prompt communication with the veterinarian about any concerns ensures that potential issues are addressed promptly. In addition to veterinary care, routine home care procedures like brushing, cleaning, and feeding a balanced food promote the general well-being and health of Pitbulls.

To sum up, routine veterinary examinations are essential to responsible Pitbull ownership and help maintain their general health, lifespan, and well-being. Regular veterinary inspections must include preventive care measures, immunizations, dental treatment, parasite management, and testing for health issues unique to a particular breed. Pitbull owners and veterinarians collaborate closely to address health issues, offer advice on preventive care, and strengthen the link between people and their devoted canine friends. Frequent veterinary examinations guarantee the physical and mental health of Pitbulls, enabling them to live happy, healthy lives as valued family members.

Choosing the Right Diet

The proper diet is essential to support their muscular build, maintain energy levels, and address specific health considerations associated with the breed. In this section, we delve into the importance of proper nutrition for Pitbulls, explore their unique dietary requirements, and provide guidance on choosing a well-balanced and suitable diet to ensure their longevity and vitality.

Pitbulls are a muscular, athletic, and devoted breed, and their nutritional requirements are crucial to their general health and well-being. They need the right food to support their muscular build, sustain their energy levels, and care for specific health issues unique to the breed. This section delves into the significance of adequate nutrition for Pitbulls, examines their particular dietary needs, and offers suggestions for selecting a healthy, well-balanced food to maintain longevity and vitality.

Pitbulls, known for their strength and tenacity, need a diet that meets their unique requirements because of their energy levels, muscle bulk, and possible health issues. Pitbulls have a more significant metabolism than other smaller or less active breeds; thus, in order to maintain their energy and general health, they may need a diet high in particular nutrients. Therefore, choosing the proper diet requires being aware of the specific traits of the breed and making dietary adjustments accordingly.

The amount of protein Pitbulls need in their diet is an essential factor. Pitbulls are an athletic and muscular breed that greatly benefit from eating high-quality animal protein sources in their diet. Protein is necessary for the growth, upkeep, and repair of muscles, which supports the busy lifestyle of Pitbulls. To provide the essential amino acids required for the strength and agility of the breed, look for dog diets that have meat, chicken, or fish as the main ingredient.

Another essential part of a Pitbull's diet is fat. Although monitoring fat consumption is crucial to avoid obesity, these energetic canines benefit significantly from healthy fats as an excellent energy source. The state of the skin, the health of the coat, and overall wellbeing all depend on omega-3 and omega-6 fatty acids. Foods like flaxseed and fish oil contain them. Stabilizing the fat level of the food helps meet the energy needs of the Pitbull without changing their weight or raising their risk of health issues.

Pitbulls need carbohydrates in their diet since they are an energy source. However, it's important to choose complex carbohydrates—such as those in whole grains and vegetables—over simple ones. The Pitbull stays active without experiencing a spike in blood sugar levels thanks to the gradual release of energy from complex carbs. Pitbulls require a well-balanced diet with the right proportions of fats, proteins, and carbohydrates to thrive.

Owners of Pitbulls should be mindful of the possibility of food allergies or sensitivities while deciding on a diet. Certain Pitbulls may be more susceptible to allergies, which frequently show up as gastrointestinal, skin, or ear infections. Dog diets with fewer additives or new protein sources can help handle sensitivities. A veterinarian's advice may occasionally be required to pinpoint specific food issues and suggest appropriate hypoallergenic solutions.

Pitbull pups have different nutritional requirements than adult dogs, so their diet must promote healthy growth and development. Feeding a Pitbull premium puppy food designed for medium to large breeds in its early years is advised. These diets supply the right amounts of minerals, like phosphorus and calcium, to support the development of strong bones and muscles. As they get older, pitbulls adjust their diets to meet their changing energy requirements, and a seamless transition is crucial to their long-term health.

When choosing the proper diet for Pitbulls, it is essential to be aware of any potential health risks related to the breed. Pitbulls may be more prone to skin allergies or hip dysplasia, for example. Preventive healthcare requires food planning to treat or minimize these issues. It may be worthwhile to look into specialized dog meals designed for joint health or sensitive skin, and speaking with a veterinarian can offer essential insights into the dietary decisions that best support the Pitbull's particular health profile.

Pitbull owners often contemplate the pros and downsides of homemade diets against commercial dog food. Both solutions have advantages; the choice ultimately comes down to personal preference, financial constraints, and the dog's requirements. To ensure they fulfill nutritional criteria, premium commercial dog diets for medium- to large-breed dogs frequently undergo extensive testing. If choosing to follow a homemade diet, care must be taken to ensure that the proteins, fats, carbohydrates, and vital vitamins and minerals are balanced. Having advice from a veterinarian or a canine nutritionist can help ensure that a homemade diet is well-rounded and fits the unique requirements of a pit bull.

The raw food diet, also known as a natural or BARF diet (Biologically Appropriate Raw Food), is another option that some Pitbull owners explore. Advocates of the raw food diet believe it promotes dental health, enhances coat condition, and provides optimal nutrition. However, it's essential to approach the raw food diet cautiously, as it requires meticulous attention to hygiene, potential nutrient imbalances, and the risk of bacterial contamination. Before adopting a raw food diet, owners should thoroughly research and consult with veterinary professionals to ensure its safety and suitability for their Pitbull.

Due to their higher metabolism and muscular build, Pitbulls may have a propensity for gaining weight if overfed or given excessive treats. Weight control for dogs can be achieved through regular weight monitoring, activity-level-based portion adjustments, and a well-balanced assortment of goodies that enhance the dog's diet. Preventing obesity-related illnesses, such as joint and cardiovascular diseases, requires maintaining a healthy weight.

Drinking enough water is an essential but sometimes neglected part of a Pitbull's diet. A sufficient amount of fresh, clean water is necessary for these energetic canines to maintain their energy levels and avoid dehydration. Water should always be available throughout the day, especially after exertion. Many body processes, such as digestion, nutrition absorption, and temperature regulation, depend on enough hydration. Pit bulls' general health can be negatively impacted by dehydration. Therefore, owners should ensure their dogs always have access to water throughout the day, which is essential, especially after physical activity. Hydration is critical for various bodily functions, including digestion, nutrient absorption, and temperature regulation. Dehydration can impact a pit bull's overall well-being, so owners should consciously ensure their dogs have constant access to water.

A Pitbull's age, activity level, and overall health influence the type of diet that will best suit their needs. Adult Pitbulls engaged in regular exercise may benefit from diets designed for active or working breeds, providing the additional energy and nutrients required for their demanding physical activity. Senior Pitbulls, on the other hand, may benefit from diets tailored to address age-related concerns, such as joint health and metabolism changes. Adjusting the diet to align with the specific life stage of the Pitbull ensures that they receive the appropriate nutrition for their age and activity levels.

Regular veterinary consultations play a crucial role in ensuring that the chosen diet meets the individual needs of a Pitbull. Veterinarians can assess the dog's overall health, monitor any weight or body condition changes, and provide recommendations for dietary adjustments if necessary. Frequent examinations also make it possible to identify health problems early on that may affect a dog's nutritional needs. Maintaining open lines of contact with the veterinarian guarantees that the diet of the Pitbull is constantly adjusted to suit its changing health requirements.

In conclusion, selecting the proper diet for Pitbulls is a complex process that necessitates giving serious thought to all of their unique traits, age, degree of activity, and possible health issues. Owners need to be aware of the special nutritional needs of their breed, keep an eye on portion amounts, and modify their diets according to their activity and age levels. Frequent visits to the vet offer priceless advice on customizing the diet to each Pitbull's unique requirements, extending their lifespan, vigor, and general well-being.

Common Health Issues in Pitbulls

Pitbulls, renowned for their strength, loyalty, and affectionate nature, are robust dogs known for their overall resilience. However, like any other breed, Pitbulls may be predisposed to specific health issues that owners should be aware of to ensure their well-being. In this post, we'll look at a few common health problems that Pitbulls face and their causes, symptoms, and management techniques that can help these cherished canine friends live long, healthy lives.

Hip dysplasia, a genetic disorder that can impair the hip joints, is a common health issue among Pitbulls. Hip dysplasia is a condition with wear and tear on the hip joint because it does not fit tightly into the hip socket. Hip dysplasia is genetic, but environmental factors like quick growth or significant weight gain can worsen the condition. Hip dysplasia is frequently accompanied by decreased activity, stair resistance, or a discernible alteration in stride. Pitbulls who take preventive steps, including regular exercise, joint supplements, and proper weight maintenance, can lessen the effects of hip dysplasia.

Skin allergies are another health issue that can affect Pitbulls, causing discomfort and irritation. Allergies may result from various factors, including environmental triggers like pollen or dust mites, certain foods, or irritant contact. Pitbulls with skin allergies frequently experience itching, redness, hair loss, and repeated ear infections as symptoms. Manage and avoid allergic reactions by identifying and removing the allergen by dietary modifications, environmental control, or allergy testing. Regular grooming, such as washing and brushing, helps Pitbulls' skin stay healthy and prevent skin-related problems.

Pitbulls are more likely to have cardiac problems, aortic stenosis being one of the more common ones. While symptoms aren't always evident, severe cases might cause exercise intolerance, cardiac murmurs, and fainting. Early detection and treatment of cardiac disorders are made possible by routine veterinarian examinations, which include cardiac screenings. Depending on the severity of the problem, recommendations for medications or surgical procedures may be made, which will improve the quality of life for Pitbulls with heart problems.

Deafness is a health issue that can affect some Pitbulls, with a genetic predisposition in specific coat colors, such as white. Congenital deafness is present at birth and affected Pitbulls may display behaviors such as not responding to sounds or having difficulty waking up. While deafness cannot be cured, training techniques using visual or tactile cues can help owners communicate effectively with their deaf Pitbulls. Early detection and positive reinforcement training contribute to a fulfilling life for Pitbulls with congenital deafness, allowing them to adapt and thrive in their environment.

Pitbulls may get cataracts, cloudings of the eye's lens that impair vision. Pitbulls may be predisposed to early-onset cataracts by specific genetic variables, even though cataracts may develop with age. Some symptoms include a foggy appearance in the eye, trouble seeing in dim light, or behavioral abnormalities. Pitbulls who have cataracts can have them surgically removed to restore their vision. To preserve ocular health and reduce the development of cataracts in Pitbulls, routine eye exams and preventive actions like shielding the eyes from trauma are essential.

Pitbulls frequently experience orthopedic problems related to cruciate ligament injuries, particularly the cranial cruciate ligament rupture (CCL). Because the CCL stabilizes the knee joint, damage can result from trauma, obesity, or inherited tendencies. A cruciate ligament damage may manifest as a limp, pain when bearing weight on the injured leg or swelling surrounding the knee joint. Depending on the extent of the damage, management options include physical therapy, rest, or surgery. They are Keeping pit bulls at a healthy weight, exercising frequently, and avoiding excessive jumping or demanding activities, all of which help to prevent cruciate ligament injury.

Certain Pitbulls may be predisposed to skin conditions such as demodectic mange caused by the Demodex mite. While these mites are commonly present on the skin, an overgrowth can led to skin inflammation and hair loss. Weak immune systems, genetics, or stress can contribute to developing demodectic mange. Symptoms include bald patches, redness, and skin lesions. Treatment involves addressing the underlying cause, boosting the immune system, and managing symptoms with medicated shampoos or medications a veterinarian prescribes. Regular skin checks and a balanced diet contribute to preventing and managing demodectic mange in Pitbulls.

Pitbulls may be affected by A condition referred to as hypothyroidism, in which the thyroid gland is unable to produce enough hormones, which can result in several health problems. Hypothyroidism can cause changes in skin texture, weight gain, tiredness, and hair loss. As part of standard veterinary examinations, thyroid function tests enable the early detection and treatment of hypothyroidism. To treat the hormonal imbalance and improve the Pitbull's general health, thyroid hormone replacement therapy is used.

While these health issues are among the more common concerns for Pitbulls, it's essential to emphasize that individual dogs may have unique health profiles. Regular veterinary check-ups are instrumental in assessing the overall health of Pitbulls, allowing for early detection and intervention when necessary. Owners must watch for changes in their pet's eating habits, demeanor, or general health. They should contact their veterinarian straight away if they have any concerns.

Preventive healthcare measures are crucial when it comes to managing and lessening the consequences of common health issues in pit bulls. Maintaining a healthy weight involves eating a balanced diet, exercising frequently, and considering specific breed-specific characteristics. Good grooming practices, dental health, and parasite prevention contribute to well-being. Responsible ownership includes understanding the breed's unique characteristics, staying informed about any health issues, and actively participating in preventive healthcare.

In conclusion, owners should be aware of potential health hazards for their pets, even though Pitbulls are generally robust and resilient dogs. Early intervention, preventive healthcare measures, and regular veterinary check-ups are crucial to address and manage common health issues in Pitbulls. Responsible ownership includes feeding a balanced and proper diet, being aware of breed-specific difficulties, and considering each Pitbull's individual health needs. When given the appropriate care and attention, pitbulls may live long, healthy lives and are outstanding family members.

CHAPTER IX

Grooming and Care

Bathing and Brushing

Pitbulls, known for their strength, intelligence, and affectionate nature, require regular grooming to maintain optimal hygiene and a healthy coat. Bathing and brushing are integral components of a Pitbull's care routine, contributing to their physical well-being and fostering a strong bond between owners and their loyal canine companions. In this essay, we delve into the importance of bathing and brushing for Pitbulls, explore the frequency and techniques involved, and discuss the benefits that extend beyond aesthetics to encompass skin health and overall happiness.

Bathing is a crucial aspect of Pitbull grooming, helping to keep their skin clean and free from dirt, debris, and potential allergens. Contrary to common misconceptions, Pitbulls do not require frequent baths, as their short coat and natural oils contribute to a self-cleaning mechanism. However, periodic baths are essential to address specific needs, such as removing accumulated dirt, minimizing odors, and managing skin conditions.

The frequency of Pitbull baths depends on various factors, including the dog's activity level, exposure to outdoor elements, and individual skin conditions. Typically, Pitbulls benefit from baths every 6 to 8 weeks or as needed. Overexposure to the sun can deplete the coat's natural oils, causing dryness and possibly even skin problems. However, skipping frequent baths can lead to a buildup of debris and bacteria, which may irritate your skin. By finding the right mix depending on each dog's unique needs, Pitbulls can keep their skin healthy and robust without sacrificing the natural oils that protect it.

It is imperative to use a dog-friendly shampoo designed exclusively for the coat type of your Pitbull before bathing it. Their skin's natural equilibrium might be upset by harsh or human shampoos, which can cause dryness or discomfort. Pitbulls do best with mild, hypoallergenic shampoos made for delicate skin. Towels, a non-slip mat, and an appropriate dog brush are among the items that should be gathered to ensure that bath time is easy and stress-free for both the dog and the owner.

After thoroughly wetting the pit bull's coat, the shampoo is applied, and the coat is massaged to ensure even application. Pay close attention to delicate parts like the paws and tummy is essential. Rinsing thoroughly is necessary to eliminate all shampoo residue and avoid irritating the skin. After bathing, owners should ensure their Pitbull is completely dry with a towel to prevent any moisture that could aggravate skin conditions. In addition to helping to disperse natural oils and eliminate loose hair, brushing the coat while it dries helps to create a glossy, healthy coat.

Brushing is equally essential for Pitbulls, despite their short coat. While Pitbulls do not have the long, dense fur seen in some breeds, they do shed, and regular brushing helps manage shedding, remove loose hair, and prevent matting. Additionally, brushing stimulates the skin and promotes blood circulation, contributing to a healthier coat and overall skin condition.

Choosing the right brush for a Pitbull is critical to effective grooming. Slicker brushes or rubber grooming mitts work well for Pitbulls, helping to remove loose hair and distribute natural oils. Regular brushing, ideally done once or twice a week, contributes to a cleaner coat, reduces shedding, and allows owners to monitor the skin for any signs of irritation, lumps, or abnormalities.

Pitbulls are not known for being particularly prone to matting or tangles, but regular brushing is essential to remove dead hair and prevent the buildup of loose fur around the house. This is especially crucial during seasonal shedding periods when Pitbulls may experience increased hair loss. Consistent brushing helps manage shedding and keeps the coat looking sleek and healthy.

Beyond the aesthetic benefits, both bathing and brushing contribute to the overall well-being of Pitbulls. Regular brushing fosters a positive physical connection between owners and their dogs, providing an opportunity for bonding and reinforcing trust. This is particularly important for Pitbulls, known for their loyalty and affectionate nature. Grooming sessions become moments of shared care and attention, enhancing the emotional bond between the owner and their Pitbull.

Bathing also plays a role in maintaining a Pitbull's skin health. While their short coat requires less maintenance than longer-haired breeds, regular baths help prevent skin issues such as fungal or bacterial infections. Drying the Pitbull thoroughly after a bath is essential to avoid dampness, which can create an environment conducive to skin problems. Additionally, bathing allows owners to inspect the Pitbull's skin for any indications of sensitivity, redness, or abnormalities that may require veterinary attention.

Grooming sessions also allow checking other aspects of a Pitbull's health. Owners can inspect the ears for signs of infection, check the teeth and gums for dental health, and examine the paws for any cuts, foreign objects, or signs of discomfort. The holistic approach to grooming allows owners to address potential health issues early, contributing to the overall well-being of their Pitbull.

It is crucial to approach grooming with patience and positive reinforcement, mainly if a Pitbull is not accustomed to the process. Starting grooming routines from a young age helps acclimate Pitbulls to the experience and fosters a positive association with bathing and brushing. Using treats, praise, and a calm demeanor during grooming sessions helps create a positive and stress-free environment, ensuring that Pitbulls view grooming as a pleasant and bonding experience.

In conclusion, bathing and brushing are essential components of Pitbull care, contributing to their physical health and hygiene and the emotional bond between owners and their loyal canine companions. The frequency of baths should be tailored to individual needs, avoiding over-bathing while addressing specific cleanliness and skin health concerns. Despite their short coat, regular brushing helps manage shedding, promotes a healthy coat and skin, and allows owners to monitor their Pitbull's overall health. Grooming sessions become moments of shared care and attention, strengthening the emotional connection between Pitbulls and their owners. Approaching grooming with patience, positive reinforcement, and a gentle touch ensures that Pitbulls associate the experience with comfort, contributing to a happy and well-maintained canine companion.

Nail Trimming

Nail trimming is an often overlooked yet crucial aspect of grooming for Pitbulls, a breed celebrated for its strength, loyalty, and distinctive appearance. Proper nail care supports Pitbulls' comfort, mobility, and general health. This section delves into the importance of nail cutting for Pitbulls, examines the difficulties involved in this grooming chore, and offers recommendations on methods and frequency to guarantee a happy and stress-free experience for owners and their furry friends.

Like many dog breeds, Pitbulls have constantly growing nails. Therefore, routine cutting is required to avoid discomfort, problems with mobility, and possible health issues. Long nails can affect how a pit bull walks, leading to imbalanced weight distribution and joint issues. Additionally, splitting or breaking overgrown nails could cause pain and possibly infections. For this reason, nail cutting is a crucial part of a Pitbull's regular grooming regimen that helps to preserve their general well-being.

The frequency of nail trimming for Pitbulls depends on various factors, including the dog's activity level, environment, and individual nail growth rate. Typically, nails should be checked and trimmed every 2 to 4 weeks. Dogs that spend more time indoors or on softer surfaces may require more frequent nail maintenance, while those with more outdoor activity on more complex surfaces may naturally wear down their nails to some extent. Regular monitoring of the nails allows owners to gauge when trimming is necessary and prevents the development of long, curved nails that can lead to discomfort.

One challenge associated with nail trimming for Pitbulls is their strong and sometimes apprehensive nature. Some Pitbulls may be resistant to having their paws handled or may display anxiety during the trimming process. This can make the task challenging for both first-time and experienced owners. Therefore, it is essential to approach nail trimming with patience, positive reinforcement, and a gradual introduction to the process.

Introducing Pitbulls to nail trimming from a young age helps them become accustomed to the experience and fosters a positive association. Starting with short sessions of handling the paws, offering treats and praise, and gradually introducing the sound and sensation of the nail clippers or grinder contribute to a positive and stress-free environment. Consistency and positive reinforcement help build trust between owners and Pitbulls, making future nail trimming sessions more manageable.

Choosing the right tools for nail trimming is crucial for a successful and stress-free experience. Nail clippers or grinders specifically designed for dogs are readily available, each with advantages. Guillotine-style clippers are efficient for smaller nails, while scissor-style clippers or grinders offer precision and control. It is crucial to use instruments suitable for the size and thickness of a Pitbull's nails to ensure safe and effective trimming.

The quick blood vessels and nerves inside the nail are primary considerations during trimming. The short is often visible in light-colored nails as a pinkish area, making it easier for owners to gauge how much to trim. However, the prompt may need to be more visual in dark-colored nails, requiring extra caution. Trimming small amounts at a time and using a bright light to illuminate the quick can help prevent accidentally cutting into it.

Nail grinders are an alternative tool for Pitbull nail care, offering a gentler approach to trimming. Grinder's file down the nails gradually, reducing the risk of cutting into the quick. They also provide a smoother finish, minimizing the potential for sharp edges. While some Pitbulls may take time to acclimate to the noise and vibration of a grinder, many find it less intimidating than traditional clippers. Consistency in the grinder helps dogs become familiar with the process, making subsequent sessions more comfortable.

Owners must observe signs indicating a Pitbull's nails need trimming. Clicking sounds when the dog walks, visible curling or crossing of the nails, and discomfort or reluctance to put weight on the paws are indications that the nails require attention. Additionally, inspecting the paws and nails during regular grooming sessions allows owners to identify any issues, such as ingrown nails or foreign objects between the toes.

In cases where owners are unsure or uncomfortable with performing nail trimming themselves, seeking the assistance of a professional groomer or veterinarian is a viable option. Groomers and veterinarians have the experience and expertise to safely trim nails, ensuring that the quick is not cut and minimizing stress for the dog and the owner. A comprehensive examination of the health of the paws may also be done during professional grooming appointments, which enables the early identification of any problems that may need to be fixed.

In addition to its obvious health benefits, nail cutting helps foster a strong bond of trust between Pitbulls and their owners. Positive reward and consistent, gentle paw handling strengthen the link between the dog and its caretaker. Because of this favorable link, Pitbulls are less likely to associate nail cutting with stress or anxiety and are more likely to see it as a regular part of grooming.

In conclusion, nail trimming is an essential aspect of Pitbull care that should not be overlooked. Regular trimming ensures the comfort, mobility, and overall health of Pitbulls by preventing issues associated with prolonged or overgrown nails. Approaching nail trimming with patience, positive reinforcement, and a gradual introduction to the process helps create a stress-free experience for both owners and Pitbulls. Consistent grooming routines from a young age foster a positive association, strengthening the emotional bond between the dog and its caregiver. Choosing the right tools, monitoring nail health, and seeking professional assistance when needed contribute to maintaining the well-being and happiness of Pitbulls through proper nail care.

Dental Care

Maintaining proper dental care for Pitbulls is vital to overall canine wellness, contributing to their oral health and general well-being. Pitbulls, known for their strength, loyalty, and affectionate nature, benefit significantly from a proactive approach to dental care. This section discusses the value of dental hygiene for Pitbulls, the difficulties in maintaining good oral hygiene, and doable methods to guarantee the longevity of good oral health.

For Pitbulls, dental health is essential because it directly impacts their quality of life. Tooth decay, gum disease, foul breath, and even systemic health disorders can be brought on by poor oral hygiene. Contrary to popular belief, dogs—including Pitbulls—can maintain good oral health independently. Routine dental care prevents dental problems that could jeopardize a dog's general well-being.

One of the primary challenges in Pitbull dental care is the breed's strong and sometimes resistant nature. Many Pitbulls may be apprehensive about having their mouths handled, making dental care tasks such as teeth brushing or inspections more challenging for owners. To overcome this challenge, it is crucial to introduce dental care routines from a young age, fostering a positive association with oral care. Starting with gentle touches, offering treats, and gradually progressing to toothbrushing helps build trust and makes dental care a more tolerable experience for Pitbulls.

Teeth brushing is a cornerstone of Pitbull dental care and is pivotal in preventing plaque and tartar buildup. Using a dog-friendly toothbrush and toothpaste is crucial, as human toothpaste can harm dogs. Owners should brush their Pitbull's teeth regularly, ideally three to four times weekly, to maintain optimal oral health. The act of brushing not only removes plaque and prevents tartar but also stimulates the gums, promoting blood circulation and contributing to healthier teeth.

Choosing an appropriate toothbrush and toothpaste is essential for effective dental care. Dog toothbrushes are designed to reach all areas of a dog's mouth, and using a toothbrush with soft bristles helps prevent damage to the gums. Dog toothpaste comes in scents that dogs like, so the owner and the Pitbull will have a better time using it. By introducing toothpaste gradually and letting the Pitbull taste it, you can establish a favorable relationship that will make cleaning your teeth easier in the future.

A Pitbull's oral health is enhanced by including dental chews or toys in their routine in addition to essential tooth brushing. Chew toys that encourage good dental hygiene promote chewing, which naturally cleans teeth and helps prevent plaque and tartar development. Dental chews designed with specific oral health issues in mind, including plaque reduction or lousy breath control, offer a fun and easy method to complement routine dental care.

Dental check-ups with a veterinarian are another critical aspect of Pitbull dental care. Regular veterinary examinations allow for professional assessments of a Pitbull's oral health, including identifying potential issues such as gum disease, tooth decay, or misalignments. Professional dental cleanings performed under anesthesia may be recommended to address more advanced dental problems. Veterinarians can also guide specific dental care needs based on the Pitbull's age, overall health, and individual oral health profile.

Periodontal disease, which entails inflammation and infection of the gums and tooth-supporting tissues, is a common dental condition in Pitbulls. The sticky film of bacteria on teeth, known as plaque, is frequently the first sign of periodontal disease. Plaque can become tartar if left unchecked, which can cause gum inflammation and, eventually, more serious dental issues. Indications of periodontal disease in Pitbulls can include foul breath, bleeding or red gums, trouble eating, or unwillingness to allow a mouth examination.

To prevent and manage periodontal disease, owners should monitor their Pitbull's oral health and seek veterinary attention if any signs of dental issues arise. In addition to teeth brushing and chews, incorporating dental rinses or water additives into a Pitbull's routine can contribute to plaque prevention and oral health. These products often contain ingredients that help combat bacteria and promote healthier gums.

Dietary choices also play a role in Pitbull dental care. Feeding a balanced and nutritious diet that includes dental-friendly components contributes to oral health. Some commercial dog foods are formulated to support dental hygiene by incorporating ingredients that reduce plaque and tartar. Additionally, avoiding excessive sugary treats and providing chewable items that promote dental health, such as raw bones, can contribute to naturally cleaning a pit bull's teeth.

Owners should be mindful of potential dental issues that may arise with age. Pitbulls may become prone to tooth decay, loss, or other dental concerns as they grow older. Regular veterinary check-ups become increasingly crucial for senior Pitbulls, as they allow early detection and intervention to address age-related dental issues.

To sum up, dental care is an essential component of overall health for Pitbulls, contributing to their comfort, longevity, and quality of life. Owners play a pivotal role in maintaining their Pitbull's oral health through regular teeth brushing, incorporating dental chews or toys, and seeking professional veterinary care when needed. Starting dental care routines from a young age and creating positive associations with oral care tasks help make the experience more enjoyable for both the owner and the Pitbull. With consistent and proactive dental care,

Pitbulls can enjoy a lifetime of good oral health, ensuring they remain happy, healthy, and free from the discomfort of dental issues.

CHAPTER X

Pitbull Success Stories

Real-Life Stories of Well-Balanced Pitbulls

In a world often clouded by misconceptions and stereotypes surrounding Pitbulls, real-life stories of well-balanced and loving individuals from this breed have the power to challenge prevailing narratives and showcase the true nature of these remarkable dogs. Beyond the headlines and sensationalized accounts, Pitbulls have emerged as loyal, affectionate, and well-behaved companions in the lives of many families. This section aims to shed light on the real-life stories of well-balanced Pitbulls, highlighting their positive traits, dispelling myths, and emphasizing the importance of responsible ownership in fostering harmonious relationships between Pitbulls and their human families.

One such heartwarming tale revolves around Rocky, a Pitbull rescued from a challenging background of neglect and mistreatment. Despite his difficult start, Rocky defied the odds and blossomed into a well-balanced and affectionate family member. Through patient training, positive reinforcement, and unwavering love from his adoptive family, Rocky overcame past traumas and became an ambassador for Pitbulls, showcasing their resilience and capacity for love. His story exemplifies the transformative power of a caring environment and the potential for positive change in even the most challenging circumstances.

Similarly, the story of Bella, a Pitbull therapy dog, illustrates the incredible bond that can develop between Pitbulls and their human counterparts. Certified as a therapy dog, Bella regularly visits hospitals, nursing homes, and schools, bringing joy and comfort to individuals facing various challenges. Her gentle demeanor, intuitive nature, and love for human interaction have touched the lives of those she meets and challenged stereotypes surrounding Pitbulls. Bella's story exemplifies the potential for Pitbulls to become compassionate and empathetic companions, positively impacting the communities they serve.

Another remarkable tale involves Max, a Pitbull mix rescued from a shelter, who became a certified search and rescue dog. Max's intelligence, agility, and strong work ethic made him an ideal candidate for search and rescue missions, where he played a crucial role in locating missing individuals and providing solace to those in distress. Max's story showcases the versatility of Pitbulls and their ability to excel in various roles when supplied with the proper training, care, and opportunities. His contributions to search and rescue efforts saved lives and challenged prevailing stereotypes about Pitbulls' capabilities.

In the realm of family life, the story of Luna, a Pitbull adopted by a family with young children, paints a picture of a loving and protective canine companion. Luna seamlessly integrated into the family dynamic, forming strong bonds with the children and becoming a source of joy and comfort. Her playful and affectionate nature dispelled any concerns about Pitbulls being incompatible with families, emphasizing the breed's potential for being gentle and loving members of households with children. Luna's story highlights the importance of responsible ownership, socialization, and positive reinforcement in nurturing well-balanced Pitbulls.

The narrative of Ace, a Pitbull trained as a service dog, showcases the breed's intelligence and adaptability in assisting individuals with disabilities. Ace's training included tasks such as retrieving items, providing support during mobility challenges, and offering emotional comfort. His story challenges stereotypes by illustrating how Pitbulls, when given the proper guidance and training, can become invaluable service animals, enhancing the quality of life for individuals with diverse needs. Ace's journey exemplifies the breed's potential to serve as dedicated and reliable companions in various capacities.

These real-life stories collectively underline the importance of responsible ownership, proper training, and positive reinforcement in shaping the behavior of Pitbulls. Despite their unique backgrounds and experiences, each of these dogs flourished in environments where they were provided with love, care, and structured guidance. These stories serve as a reminder that Pitbulls, like any other breed, thrive when treated with kindness, respect, and understanding.

It is crucial to acknowledge that any dog's behavior, including Pitbulls, is influenced by a combination of genetics, environment, and individual experiences. Responsible ownership entails providing appropriate training, socialization, and care to ensure that Pitbulls develop into well-balanced and well-mannered companions. The stories of Rocky, Bella, Max, Luna, and Ace demonstrate that positive outcomes are achievable when owners invest time, effort, and compassion into fostering a strong bond with their Pitbulls.

Dispelling stereotypes surrounding Pitbulls is an ongoing effort that requires education, advocacy, and a focus on individual stories that showcase the breed's positive qualities. While it is essential to acknowledge that no breed is entirely free from unique variations in behavior, perpetuating negative stereotypes based on breed alone does a disservice to the many well-behaved and loving Pitbulls that enrich the lives of their families.

Ultimately, the real-life stories of well-balanced Pitbullsdispel myths provide a more complex explanation of the breed. These stories emphasize the importance of responsible ownership, positive reinforcement, and the transformative power of love and care in shaping the behavior of Pitbulls. By celebrating the positive traits and accomplishments of Pitbulls in various roles, from therapy dogs to service animals, we can contribute to a more compassionate and informed perspective on this misunderstood breed. Realizing the potential for well-balanced and loving relationships with Pitbulls requires a shift in perception that focuses on each dog's individuality and the positive impact they can have when provided with the right environment and guidance.

Overcoming Challenges

Taking in a Pitbull, often perceived as a challenge due to prevailing stereotypes and misconceptions surrounding the breed, can be a transformative journey marked by compassion, understanding, and the breaking down of barriers. Many individuals and families who have chosen to open their hearts and homes to Pitbulls have discovered the incredible resilience, loyalty, and affection these dogs can offer. In this section, we explore the challenges faced by those who decide to adopt Pitbulls, the rewards of overcoming stereotypes, and the positive transformations that occur when these misunderstood dogs are given a chance to thrive in loving environments.

One primary challenge individual face when adopting Pitbulls is the stigma associated with the breed. Pitbulls have long been subject to negative stereotypes, often portrayed as aggressive or dangerous dogs in the media. This stigma can create hurdles for potential adopters, as they may encounter prejudice from friends, family, or even neighbors who hold ingrained beliefs about Pitbulls. Overcoming these preconceptions requires patience, education, and a commitment to challenging misconceptions through positive interactions with the adopted Pitbull.

A crucial aspect of overcoming challenges in adopting a Pitbull is understanding the breed's history and acknowledging the impact of irresponsible ownership on its reputation. Pitbulls, initially bred for various purposes, including farm work and as family companions, were unfortunately later exploited in dog fighting. As a result, some Pitbulls may have experienced neglect, abuse, or improper training, contributing to behavioral challenges. Adopters can overcome initial challenges by recognizing the breed's historical context and providing a nurturing environment.

Behavioral issues may be prevalent in Pitbulls with challenging pasts, but with patience, consistent training, and positive reinforcement, these challenges can be addressed. Many Pitbulls that have faced adversity respond well to love, structure, and guidance. Adopters are willing to invest time building a strong bond and trust with their Pitbull and often witness remarkable behavioral transformations. This process benefits the individual dog and contributes to dispelling myths about the breed's inherent aggression.

Socialization is another critical aspect of overcoming challenges when adopting a Pitbull. Properly introducing a Pitbull to various environments, people, and other animals helps them develop positive social behaviors and reduces anxiety or fear-based reactions. Socialization not only addresses potential behavioral challenges but also contributes to fostering a confident and balanced canine companion.

One significant challenge faced by adopters of Pitbulls is navigating breed-specific legislation (BSL), which imposes restrictions or bans on owning certain breeds, including Pitbulls, in certain regions. BSL is often rooted in stereotypes and misinformation, targeting breeds rather than addressing the root causes of dog-related incidents. Overcoming BSL involves advocating for evidence-based, breed-neutral legislation focusing on responsible ownership, education, and community safety. Many individuals who have taken in Pitbulls become vocal advocates for fair and humane treatment, working towards the repeal or amendment of discriminatory breed-specific laws.

The rewards of overcoming challenges in adopting a Pitbull are multifaceted and deeply fulfilling. Adopters often find themselves forging unbreakable bonds with their Pitbulls, experiencing a level of loyalty and affection that challenges the negative stereotypes associated with the breed. Pitbulls, known for their innate desire to please their owners, thrive in environments where they receive love, positive reinforcement, and clear guidance. The transformation from a misunderstood and potentially troubled dog to a beloved family member is a testament to the resilience and inherent goodness of Pitbulls.

In many cases, Pitbulls that have overcome challenges through adoption become ambassadors for the breed, dispelling stereotypes through positive interactions and community engagement. Adopters who share their success stories become advocates for responsible ownership and breed education, fostering a more compassionate understanding of Pitbulls. These transformed Pitbulls, once overlooked or misunderstood, become living proof that love, patience, and positive reinforcement can reshape their behavior and break down the barriers erected by stereotypes.

The impact of overcoming challenges in adopting a Pitbull extends beyond the individual dog and adoptive family. It contributes to the larger narrative surrounding the breed, challenging societal perceptions and fostering a more inclusive and informed perspective. As more individuals open their homes to Pitbulls and share their positive experiences, the collective effort contributes to changing the narrative around these dogs, advocating for their fair treatment, and dispelling the myths that have unfairly tarnished their reputation.

In conclusion, taking in a Pitbull is a journey marked by challenges, compassion, and transformation. Overcoming the stigma associated with the breed, addressing potential behavioral issues, navigating breed-specific legislation, and advocating for fair treatment are all part of the process. The rewards, however, are immeasurable—forging deep connections with a loving and loyal companion, dispelling stereotypes through positive interactions, and contributing to a more compassionate and informed understanding of Pitbulls. Each adopted Pitbull represents a triumph over adversity, a testament to the power of love and responsible ownership, and an opportunity to reshape the narrative surrounding this misunderstood breed.

Celebrating the Bond Between Pitbulls and Owners

The bond between Pitbulls and their owners is evidence of the deep relationship that can be forged between humans and these often-misunderstood dogs. In a world where stereotypes and misconceptions about Pitbulls persist, countless stories abound of the unwavering loyalty, love, and companionship that define the relationships between these remarkable dogs and their dedicated owners. This section explores the unique qualities that make the bond between Pitbulls and owners special, delving into the challenges faced, the rewards reaped, and the enduring nature of a connection that transcends societal stereotypes.

Pitbulls, known for their strength, agility, and affectionate nature, form powerful bonds with their owners. The loyalty exhibited by Pitbulls is often described by owners as unparalleled, with these dogs demonstrating a deep devotion to their human companions. This loyalty is evident in how Pitbulls seek to please their owners, eagerly responding to commands and exhibiting a strong desire to be an integral part of their family unit.

One of the challenges inherent in celebrating the bond between Pitbulls and owners lies in the prevailing stereotypes that unfairly characterize these dogs as inherently aggressive or dangerous. Despite these stereotypes, owners who have experienced the companionship of Pitbulls understand the stark contrast between popular perceptions and the reality of their loving and affectionate nature. Overcoming societal biases requires owners to be advocates for the breed, dispelling myths through positive interactions and sharing their personal stories of the deep bond they share with their Pitbulls.

The rewards of celebrating the bond between Pitbulls and owners are multifaceted, encompassing emotional, physical, and psychological well-being for both parties. Owners often describe a unique sense of companionship and understanding beyond the surface level. Pitbulls are known for their ability to tune into the emotions of their owners, providing comfort during difficult times and celebrating moments of joy. This emotional connection contributes to a sense of security and mutual support, fostering an environment where the Pitbull and the owner thrive emotionally.

The physical aspect of the bond between Pitbulls and owners is evident in the active lifestyle often shared by these pairs. This shared physical activity promotes the Pitbull's health and well-being and strengthens the bond between owner and dog. The mutual enjoyment of outdoor pursuits creates lasting memories and reinforces the sense of partnership that defines the relationship.

Psychologically, the bond between Pitbulls and their owners offers a sense of purpose and companionship. Pitbulls are known for their intuitive nature, and many owners describe a unique form of communication that goes beyond words. Whether it's a knowing glance, a wagging tail, or a comforting nuzzle, Pitbulls have a way of expressing their love and understanding in ways that resonate deeply with their owners. This psychological connection fosters a sense of fulfillment and joy, contributing to the overall well-being of both the Pitbull and the owner.

Celebrating the bond between Pitbulls and owners often involves overcoming challenges related to breed-specific legislation and discriminatory policies. Many regions impose restrictions or bans on owning Pitbulls, perpetuating the negative stereotypes that surround the breed. Owners who celebrate their bond with Pitbulls become advocates for fair treatment, actively participating in efforts to challenge breed-specific legislation and promote responsible ownership. By sharing their positive experiences, owners contribute to changing societal perceptions and fostering a more inclusive understanding of pit bulls.

Countless stories of resilience, loyalty, and mutual growth exemplify the enduring bond between Pitbulls and owners. Pitbulls, often adopted from shelters or rescue organizations, find themselves in loving homes where they not only become cherished family members but also bring immeasurable joy and positivity. Owners celebrating this bond understand the transformative power of compassion and patience. Many Pitbulls, having overcome challenging pasts, flourish under the care and love provided by their owners, breaking free from stereotypes and blossoming into well-adjusted and content companions.

Celebrating the bond between Pitbulls and owners extends to the broader community through initiatives such as therapy dog programs, where Pitbulls offer comfort and companionship to individuals in hospitals, nursing homes, or schools. These programs highlight the breed's gentle and nurturing qualities, challenge stereotypes, and showcase the positive impact Pitbulls can have on diverse communities. Owners who participate in such programs become ambassadors for the breed, actively contributing to changing perceptions and fostering a more compassionate understanding of Pitbulls.

In conclusion, celebrating the bond between Pitbulls and their owners is a tribute to the enduring connection that defies societal stereotypes and misconceptions. Pitbulls' unique qualities of loyalty, love, and companionship contribute to a deep and meaningful bond that positively impacts the emotional, physical, and psychological well-being of the dog and the owner. By overcoming challenges, dispelling myths, and actively advocating for fair treatment, owners play a crucial role in changing the narrative surrounding Pitbulls. Each celebration of the bond becomes a powerful testament to the transformative power of love and understanding in fostering positive relationships between Pitbulls and their dedicated owners.

CONCLUSION

In conclusion, "Pitbull Harmony: The Art of Training and Understanding - Creating a Happy, Healthy, and Well-Balanced Canine Companion" stands as a beacon for pitbull enthusiasts and owners, fostering a profound understanding of this often-misunderstood breed. Through the pages of this comprehensive guide, we have embarked on a journey to debunk myths, unveil the rich history and unique characteristics of pit bulls, and explore the art of responsible ownership.

The heart of "Pitbull Harmony" lies in emphasizing positive reinforcement training techniques designed to build trust, enhance communication, and forge a deep bond between you and your pitbull. By offering practical insights into addressing common behavioral challenges, from aggression to separation anxiety, the book empowers owners to navigate the complexities of training with compassion and skill.

Beyond training, this guide delves into the broader aspects of responsible pitbull ownership. It advocates for creating a safe and enriching environment, recognizing the significance of proper nutrition, regular exercise, and routine veterinary care. The book is a holistic resource, ensuring pitbull owners are well-equipped to meet their canine companions' physical and emotional needs.

As we conclude this journey, the overarching message is harmony between perception and reality, harmony in training methods, and, most importantly, harmony in the relationship between pit bulls and their owners. By embracing the principles outlined in "Pitbull Harmony," readers are poised to create a joyful, fulfilling, and mutually enriching partnership with their pitbulls.

The book is not merely a guide; it's a celebration of the unique qualities of pitbulls and a testament to the transformative power of understanding, patience, and positive reinforcement. We hope that "Pitbull Harmony" serves as a lasting resource, empowering pitbull owners to cultivate a happy, healthy, and well-balanced companionship that transcends stereotypes and fosters a deep and enduring bond between humans and their pitbull companions.

Thank you for buying and reading/ listening to our book. If you found this book useful/ helpful please take a few minutes and leave a review on the platform where you purchased our book. Your feedback matters greatly to us.

www.ingramcontent.com/pod-product-compliance
Lightning Source LLC
LaVergne TN
LVHW012025060526
838201LV00061B/4464